GOD'S
HeaRT
FOR YOU

God's Heart For You

Devotions &
Bible Promises
for Women

JANICE THOMPSON

BARBOUR BOOKS
An Imprint of Barbour Publishing, Inc.

© 2014 by Barbour Publishing, Inc.

Print ISBN 978-1-64352-217-3

eBook Editions:
Adobe Digital Edition (.epub) 978-1-63409-052-0
Kindle and MobiPocket Edition (.prc) 978-1-63409-053-7

Published by Barbour Books, an imprint of Barbour Publishing, Inc., 1810 Barbour Drive, Uhrichsville, Ohio 44683, www.barbourbooks.com

Our mission is to inspire the world with the life-changing message of the Bible.

Member of the
Evangelical Christian
Publishers Association

Printed in the United States of America.

INTRODUCTION

God's Word is filled to the brim with amazing promises for believers, but we often overlook them. We buzz through our daily Bible reading, missing these remarkable gems altogether, or not seeing them for what they are. What a shame!

This little book focuses on ninety-three of those promises—specific words from the Lord that you can take to the bank. The Lord wants us to be strong from the inside out, and these tidbits offer the encouragement you need to keep going when you don't feel like it. On particularly difficult days, one word from the Lord can give you what you need to face giants or stay the course.

So, brace yourself! The promises you're about to read are real. They are heaven breathed and God inspired. In fact, they might just change your life.

RESCUED FROM DARKNESS

*For he has rescued us from the dominion
of darkness and brought us into the kingdom
of the Son he loves, in whom we have
redemption, the forgiveness of sins.*

COLOSSIANS 1:13–14 NIV

If you've ever tried to navigate your way through a dark space, you know the dangers of not being able to see clearly. Sure, your eyes will eventually adjust, and you might be able to distinguish objects, but crawling around in the haze can make for a pretty dismal life.

Now picture a shaft of light breaking through your darkness, illuminating your path and sending the bogeyman running. Picture yourself being lifted—physically, spiritually, and emotionally—from that once-dark place and transported to a land where you are surrounded by light on every side. That's what it's like when God rescues us from darkness. He promises to split through the bleak, dark shadows and lift us to a new place, one where His goodness and radiant light are ever-present. Oh to be rescued by the Author of Light! To be transferred to a new "kingdom," one where His Son illuminates our path. What joy!

I will lead the blind by ways they have not known, along unfamiliar paths I will guide them; I will turn the darkness into light before them and make the rough places smooth. These are the things I will do; I will not forsake them.

ISAIAH 42:16 NIV

He led them with a cloud by day and by the light of a fire by night.

PSALM 78:14 NCV

Before those people lived in darkness, but now they have seen a great light. They lived in a dark land, but a light has shined on them.

ISAIAH 9:2 NCV

GOD'S MEDICINE: A JOYFUL HEART

A joyful heart is good medicine,
but a broken spirit dries up the bones.
PROVERBS 17:22 NASB

Everyone faces painful days. Some are so bad the easiest thing would be to crawl back into bed and hide under the covers. The pain is too severe. If only a blink of the eyes could make it go away.

God doesn't have a physical medicine for the pain we endure, but He offers something even better—joy. Yes, joy! This bubbly bit of kindness from the Lord is just the medicine to pull us out of the doldrums when we're down. His joy works like a doctor-prescribed medication, but costs a lot less and has no side effects. Well, no negative side effects, anyway! Today, raise your hands to the sky and praise God for the joy He's bestowed, even if you don't feel like it.

Every day is hard for those who suffer,
but a happy heart is like a continual feast.

PROVERBS 15:15 NCV

As a tree produces fruit,
wisdom gives life to those who use it,
and everyone who uses it will be happy.

PROVERBS 3:18 NCV

Then will the lame leap like a deer,
and the mute tongue shout for joy.
Water will gush forth in the wilderness
and streams in the desert.

ISAIAH 35:6 NIV

WE CAN STAND FAST IN LIBERTY

It is for freedom that Christ has set us free.
Stand firm, then, and do not let yourselves
be burdened again by a yoke of slavery.

GALATIANS 5:1 NIV

What a wonderful promise! We can stand in complete freedom. Liberty! Oh, the joy of knowing we don't have to be in bondage any longer. Being "yoked" to sin (or addiction) is akin to being in prison. We're locked away in our cell, unable to break free. Then, suddenly, the chains are broken. Christ breaks through the prison walls and ushers us outside into ultimate freedom.

What do we have to do to earn this freedom? Nothing! Christ did it all for us on the cross. We simply have to acknowledge this gift by accepting Jesus as Lord and Savior of our lives. In that moment, liberty is ours. It begins in an instant and lasts forever. We no longer have to be "entangled" (bound up) by sin. Oh, to be set free! What a lovely promise.

Now the Lord is the Spirit, and where
the Spirit of the Lord is, there is freedom.
2 Corinthians 3:17 NIV

You, my brothers and sisters, were called to be
free. But do not use your freedom to indulge the
flesh; rather, serve one another humbly in love.
For the entire law is fulfilled in keeping this one
command: "Love your neighbor as yourself."
Galatians 5:13–14 NIV

I will walk about in freedom,
for I have sought out your precepts.
Psalm 119:45 NIV

GOD CHOSE US

*You did not choose me, but I chose you and
appointed you so that you might go and bear fruit—
fruit that will last—and so that whatever you
ask in my name the Father will give you.*

JOHN 15:16 NIV

If you've ever had to pick someone out of a police lineup, you know what it's like to stare into the faces of many and to choose one. In a sense, that's what God did for you. He saw you in your sinful state and pointed you out. He said, "I'll take that one. I will adopt her and make her my own."

How does it feel to be chosen by God? Amazing, right? When He swept us into this new life, it wasn't to prove some sort of point. It wasn't to say, "Hey, you lousy sinner, I plan to shame you before the masses to pay you back for your wicked ways!"

No, just the opposite, in fact. He extends grace and mercy. We can't help but be filled with gratitude and wonder. The Lord of all creation chose us! And He longs for us to "bear fruit" so that we can sweep others into the Kingdom as well.

For you are a people holy to the Lord your God, and the Lord has chosen you to be a people for his treasured possession, out of all the peoples who are on the face of the earth.
DEUTERONOMY 14:2 ESV

You are a chosen group of people. . . You are a holy nation. You belong to God.
1 PETER 2:9 NLV

But the anointing that you received from him abides in you, and you have no need that anyone should teach you. But as his anointing teaches you about everything, and is true, and is no lie—just as it has taught you, abide in him.
1 JOHN 2:27 ESV

ANGELS IN OUR CAMPSITE

The angel of the LORD encamps around those who fear him, and he delivers them.

PSALM 34:7 NIV

Have you ever been on a camping trip? If so, you've likely experienced the sounds of night owls, crickets, and a variety of other nocturnal creatures. Things that go bump in the night can be especially frightening when you're out in nature under a tent. You stay awake half the night, wondering if a bear will wander into your camp or if the nearby river might spill its banks and flood the whole area.

If you knew that God's angels were standing in a circle around your campsite, would you sleep better? They are, you know! He has "encamped" His angels around us, and they are ready to protect at His command. Sure, we don't spend a lot of time thinking about their presence, but that doesn't make them any less real. So, relax! Pull the covers up and get cozy. God's got this, and He has plenty of angels on hand to help.

*There the angel of the L*ORD *appeared to him in flames of fire from within a bush. Moses saw that though the bush was on fire it did not burn up.*

EXODUS 3:2 NIV

The two angels arrived at Sodom in the evening, and Lot was sitting in the gateway of the city. When he saw them, he got up to meet them and bowed down with his face to the ground.

GENESIS 19:1 NIV

And I saw a powerful angel calling in a loud voice, "Who is worthy to break the seals and open the scroll?"

REVELATION 5:2 NCV

WE CAN BE SATISFIED

Satisfy us in the morning with your unfailing love,
that we may sing for joy and be glad all our days.

PSALM 90:14 NIV

You know that feeling you get at the end of a delicious meal? You're full to the tippy-top, oozing over with contentment. Mmm! That feeling of satisfaction leaves you feeling warm and fuzzy all over.

To be satisfied in the Lord is a similar feeling, only a thousand times better. When you're truly satisfied, you're not seeking more. Or "different." There's no room for dessert, and you wouldn't want it, even if someone offered it to you. His presence is the dessert! You're pleased—and grateful—for what you have.

What joy, to live a satisfied life. No cravings. No longings. No "what ifs." Just a blissful state of realizing that all you could ever want is right in front of you. And it is, you know, because God is right there, hand extended, ushering you into His presence.

Not that I am speaking of being in need, for I have learned in whatever situation I am to be content. I know how to be brought low, and I know how to abound. In any and every circumstance, I have learned the secret of facing plenty and hunger, abundance and need. I can do all things through him who strengthens me.

PHILIPPIANS 4:11–13 ESV

But godliness with contentment is great gain, for we brought nothing into the world, and we cannot take anything out of the world. But if we have food and clothing, with these we will be content.

1 TIMOTHY 6:6–8 ESV

I have set the LORD always before me; because he is at my right hand, I shall not be shaken. Therefore my heart is glad, and my whole being rejoices; my flesh also dwells secure.

PSALM 16:8–9 ESV

OUR FAITH CAN
MOVE MOUNTAINS

"Truly I tell you, if anyone says to this mountain,
'Go, throw yourself into the sea,' and does not doubt
in their heart but believes that what they say will
happen, it will be done for them."

MARK 11:23 NIV

Mountains are beautiful to look at—from a distance. When you're on the road, trying to get from here to there, a mountain loses its appeal. It's an obstacle. Something you have to maneuver around or climb over or tunnel through. You wish it would just go away so that your journey would be easier.

Jesus told us to speak to the mountains, or obstacles, in our lives. He promises that when faith rises up inside of us, when we speak with confidence to obstacles, they will be cast into the sea. There's an interesting promise!

The next time you're faced with an obstacle that won't seem to budge, put on your faith glasses and see it through God's eyes. Then, with all of the confidence you can muster, holler to that mountain, "Hey, you! Get out of here!" Might sound childish, but that kind of faith might just clear the road in front of you!

So he said to me, "This is the word of the L<small>ORD</small> to Zerubbabel: 'Not by might nor by power, but by my Spirit,' says the L<small>ORD</small> Almighty. "What are you, mighty mountain? Before Zerubbabel you will become level ground. Then he will bring out the capstone to shouts of 'God bless it! God bless it!' "

Z<small>ECHARIAH</small> 4:6–7 <small>NIV</small>

If I have the gift of prophecy and can fathom all mysteries and all knowledge, and if I have a faith that can move mountains, but do not have love, I am nothing.

1 C<small>ORINTHIANS</small> 13:2 <small>NIV</small>

But when you ask, you must believe and not doubt, because the one who doubts is like a wave of the sea, blown and tossed by the wind. That person should not expect to receive anything from the Lord. Such a person is double-minded and unstable in all they do.

J<small>AMES</small> 1:6–8 <small>NIV</small>

A GOOD WORD CHEERS US UP

Anxiety weighs down the heart,
but a kind word cheers it up.
PROVERBS 12:25 NIV

Words are powerful. Why? Because we have a tendency to believe what we hear, even when it's coming out of our own mouths. We reinforce fears by speaking them aloud, and we garner courage by speaking courageous things out loud. In fact, our words are so powerful that one negative word can crush a friendship or marriage.

So what kind of words are you speaking over yourself and others? Words of kindness or sharp, critical ones? God didn't put us on this earth to cut others down or to offer critique. His Holy Spirit does a far better job than we could ever do, anyway. So rather than trying to "fix" people with our words, why don't we speak kindly instead? Offer encouragement. Lift spirits. That way, their hearts are more open to God's correction and direction. We shouldn't walk around in a state of anxiety, so lift your heart and your words. That feels so much better!

And hope does not put us to shame, because God's love
has been poured out into our hearts through
the Holy Spirit, who has been given to us.

ROMANS 5:5 NIV

We demolish arguments and every pretension that sets
itself up against the knowledge of God, and we take
captive every thought to make it obedient to Christ.

2 CORINTHIANS 10:5 NIV

I will not venture to speak of anything except what Christ
has accomplished through me in leading the Gentiles
to obey God by what I have said and done.

ROMANS 15:18 NIV

WE'VE BEEN ADOPTED

God decided in advance to adopt us into his own
family by bringing us to himself through Jesus
Christ. This is what he wanted to do,
and it gave him great pleasure.

EPHESIANS 1:5 NLT

Imagine you're awaiting a new baby—not one you're giving birth to, but one you're adopting. You prepare his room and gather baby clothes and toys. A sense of anticipation builds. You can't wait to add to your little family with this new life! Finally the day arrives and the baby boy is placed into your waiting arms. You can't help but celebrate. He's now one of the family!

That's how God must feel when He adopts us into His family. He waits, as a patient Father, for us to link arms and hearts with Him. Then, as we are ushered into the family, all the "stuff" (promises in His Word) becomes ours, in much the same way that a baby is clothed and fed by his adoptive parents. God derives great pleasure out of adopting us. What joy to be included in His eternal family!

For all who are led by the Spirit of God are children of God. So you have not received a spirit that makes you fearful slaves. Instead, you received God's Spirit when he adopted you as his own children. Now we call him, "Abba, Father." For his Spirit joins with our spirit to affirm that we are God's children.

ROMANS 8:14–16 NLT

But to all who believed him and accepted him, he gave the right to become children of God.

JOHN 1:12 NLT

See what great love the Father has lavished on us, that we should be called children of God! And that is what we are! The reason the world does not know us is that it did not know him. Dear friends, now we are children of God, and what we will be has not yet been made known. But we know that when Christ appears, we shall be like him, for we shall see him as he is.

1 JOHN 3:1–2 NIV

WE HAVE FELLOWSHIP WITH GOD

God is faithful, who has called
you into fellowship with his
Son, Jesus Christ our Lord.
1 CORINTHIANS 1:9 NIV

Have you ever unpacked the word "fellowship"? It's a peculiar word, isn't it? Are we called to "ship" with our fellow man, or is there something deeper? The "ship" part actually comes from the word *companionship,* which puts things in better perspective. We're instructed to have companionship with our fellow man—or woman. "Companions" are those friends who stick pretty close. They know what we're going through even when we don't say a word.

Today's scripture is an amazing biblical promise: God has called us to fellowship (to have companionship) with the very best friend of all, Jesus. Our Savior knows us so well that He doesn't even have to ask when we're going through a rough day. He's right there, ready to dry our tears and give us strength—and courage!—to put one foot in front of the other.

Jesus is our companion. Wow! What a blessed privilege.

Jesus said, "The one who loves Me will obey My teaching. My Father will love him. We will come to him and live with him."
JOHN 14:23 NLV

We proclaim to you what we ourselves have actually seen and heard so that you may have fellowship with us. And our fellowship is with the Father and with his Son, Jesus Christ.
1 JOHN 1:3 NLT

May the grace of the Lord Jesus Christ, and the love of God, and the fellowship of the Holy Spirit be with you all.
2 CORINTHIANS 13:14 NIV

I CAN LIVE A SALTY LIFE

*"You are the salt of the earth. But if the salt loses
its saltiness, how can it be made salty again?
It is no longer good for anything, except to
be thrown out and trampled underfoot."*

MATTHEW 5:13 NIV

Many women don't see themselves as difference-makers. They're so busy changing diapers, mopping floors, driving back and forth to work, trying to catch up on sleep, and making meals that they wonder if their lives count for much at all.

What a wonderful promise from God, that we can, and will, be salt for those who need "flavor" in their lives. What does this mean? Our day-in, day-out routines might seem mundane to us, but others are watching our dedication to God, family, and friends. Their lives are being flavored by our faithful walk. When we give up, we lose our saltiness. We lose our impact.

So ask God to refill your saltshaker today. He will be happy to do it!

Let your speech always be gracious, seasoned with salt,
so that you may know how you ought
to answer each person.

COLOSSIANS 4:6 ESV

"Salt is good, but if the salt has lost its saltiness,
how will you make it salty again? Have salt in yourselves,
and be at peace with one another."

MARK 9:50 ESV

For by grace you have been saved through faith.
And this is not your own doing; it is the gift of God,
not a result of works, so that no one may boast.
For we are his workmanship, created in Christ Jesus
for good works, which God prepared beforehand,
that we should walk in them.

EPHESIANS 2:8–10 ESV

I CAN DO IT!

Do not merely listen to the word, and so deceive
yourselves. Do what it says. Anyone who listens to
the word but does not do what it says is like
someone who looks at his face in a mirror and,
after looking at himself, goes away and
immediately forgets what he looks like.

JAMES 1:22–24 NIV

We live in such a hectic world. Things swirl around us at an alarming rate. We're inundated by voices—from the television, Hollywood, family members, church friends—you name it. Sometimes it's hard to know which voices are speaking truth and which are not. That's why, when we do hear the pure message of God's truth ringing through, it's important not only to hear, but to do.

We're promised in the Word of God that we are capable of sticking with it. We don't have to glance in the mirror and then immediately forget what we look like. We can read the Word of God, absorb the Word of God, and live the Word of God. It's doable. And this heavenly "stick-to-it-iveness" means we can see each project, and each challenge, from start to finish. Whew! Now, there's good news!

And whatever you do, in word or deed, do everything in the name of the Lord Jesus, giving thanks to God the Father through him.
COLOSSIANS 3:17 ESV

And let us not grow weary of doing good, for in due season we will reap, if we do not give up.
GALATIANS 6:9 ESV

And let us consider how to stir up one another to love and good works.
HEBREWS 10:24 ESV

GOD CAN MAKE
MY HEART GLAD

*You have put gladness in my heart,
more than in the season that
their grain and wine increased.*

PSALM 4:7 NKJV

Don't you love this promise in God's Word? He can
make our hearts glad, more so than when we're walking
in full financial and emotional abundance. That means
He's capable of bringing great joy even when we are
walking through painful seasons. Hard to imagine, but
it's true. In the midst of illness or the loss of a loved one,
He can put joy in our heart.

What season are you in right now? Lacking? Plenty?
It doesn't make any difference to God. He's still capable
of giving you everything you need—not just to survive,
but to thrive. When your heart is filled with joy, you are
energized, strengthened from the inside out. And here's
the best news of all. This joy comes as a free gift. You
don't have to earn it. You don't have to beg for it. Just

reach out and grab it, then watch as you are strengthened for the days ahead.

Rejoice in the Lord always;
again I will say, rejoice.
PHILIPPIANS 4:4 ESV

May the God of hope fill you with
all joy and peace in believing,
so that by the power of the Holy Spirit
you may abound in hope.
ROMANS 15:13 ESV

Therefore my heart is glad,
and my whole being rejoices;
my flesh also dwells secure.
PSALM 16:9 ESV

GOD IS MY DWELLING PLACE

"The eternal God is your refuge,
and underneath are the everlasting arms;
He will thrust out the enemy from
before you, and will say, 'Destroy!' "

DEUTERONOMY 33:27 NKJV

We all have a picture in our head of the ultimate dream home—the place we would love to dwell. Our "safe" place. Maybe we'll never get to live in the lavish house of our imagination, but there's a dwelling place that's safer than any neighborhood or gated community. Best of all, it doesn't cost us a penny.

The very safest, and most luxurious, place to dwell is under God's wings. Wondering how you get there? Spend time in His presence. In that place, He provides comfort, security, joy, peace, and all of the other things you need.

But wait. There's more! In this amazing place, God serves as your defender. He pushes the enemy away, and you are surrounded by a vast army of angels, ready to rush to your defense. Now that is a home worth waiting for!

Now I saw a new heaven and a new earth,
for the first heaven and the first earth had
passed away. Also there was no more sea.

REVELATION 21:1 NKJV

How beautiful are the places where You live, O Lord of
all! My soul wants and even becomes weak from wanting
to be in the house of the Lord. My heart and my
flesh sing for joy to the living God.

PSALM 84:1–2 NLV

Lord, You have been our dwelling place in all
generations. Before the mountains were brought forth,
or ever You had formed the earth and the world,
even from everlasting to everlasting, You are God.

PSALM 90:1–2 NKJV

WE ARE DEAD NO MORE

"Truly, truly, I say to you, he who hears
My word, and believes Him who sent Me,
has eternal life, and does not come into judgment,
but has passed out of death into life."

JOHN 5:24 NASB

If you've ever been to a funeral, you know the deep, agonizing grief that goes along with staring at the lifeless body in the casket. Nothing feels more final than observing a once-living, once-breathing human being lying breathless and still. Now, imagine the unthinkable happens! You're leaning over, saying your goodbyes, when a gasp sounds from the body in the casket. A rush of air escapes his lungs and your friend stirs to life then sits up and greets you. Wow! Can you even imagine the joy?

That same joy rollicks the angels in heaven every time God breathes life into one of His children. When you're born again—when you accept Jesus Christ as Lord and Savior—God snaps you back to life. Eternal life, no less! You wave goodbye to death, and dance your way out of the proverbial casket, singing a song of praise. What a celebration!

> *"Go, stand in the temple courts," he said,*
> *"and tell the people all about this new life."*
> ACTS 5:20 NIV

> *Turn my eyes away from things that have no worth,*
> *and give me new life because of Your ways.*
> PSALM 119:37 NLV

> *We were therefore buried with him through baptism*
> *into death in order that, just as Christ was raised from*
> *the dead through the glory of the Father,*
> *we too may live a new life.*
> ROMANS 6:4 NIV

GOD WILL WORK IT FOR MY GOOD

And we know that in all things
God works for the good of those who
love him, who have been called
according to his purpose.

ROMANS 8:28 NIV

What a marvelous promise in this scripture! God will work all things for good. Not some things. Not the obvious things. Not the pleasant, happy things. All things. That means He will take your messes, your frustrations, your pains, your anger, the abuses others have dished out, and use them (Somehow! Miraculously!) for His glory.

Sound impossible? It's not. In fact, the Lord has already begun that work, even now. Stop for a minute and think about the things you've been through in your life. Would you be the person you are today if you hadn't walked through the deep valleys as well as the lush gardens? Can you see how God has already used your pains and your hurts to develop your character? To draw you closer to Him? Whatever you're going through right now—this very moment—rest assured, God will work it for your good, as long as your heart belongs to Him.

For it is God who works in you to will
and to act in order to fulfill his good purpose.
PHILIPPIANS 2:13 NIV

Your ears will hear a word behind you, saying,
"This is the way, walk in it," whenever you
turn to the right or to the left.
ISAIAH 30:21 NLV

"I will make you into a great nation, and I will bless you;
I will make your name great, and you will be a blessing."
GENESIS 12:2 NIV

GOD ISN'T WITHHOLDING ANYTHING FROM US

For the LORD God is a sun and shield; the LORD bestows favor and honor; no good thing does he withhold from those whose walk is blameless.

PSALM 84:11 NIV

If you've ever accumulated credit card debt, you know the sick feeling in the stomach that accompanies it. An unrighteous creditor will take you for all you're worth, charging interest rates that are out of this world. When you're bound up with this sort of debt it affects everything, including your ability to borrow for major purchases like a house or a car.

Aren't you glad that God doesn't stop the flow of blessings in your life when you mess up? He bestows favor and honor and doesn't withhold from those whose walk is blameless. Sure, we're not perfect, but as long as we ask for forgiveness for our mess-ups, He's right there, ready to offer it. And once we're forgiven, we can count on His favor. We can also count on the fact that He "shields" us from evil, which is a good thing, because we need His protection to avoid going back down the road we once traveled. Count on it! God's not cheating you out of any good thing!

"I will bless you. . .and you will be a blessing."
GENESIS 12:2 NIV

From everyone who has been given much, much will be demanded; and from the one who has been entrusted with much, much more will be asked.
LUKE 12:48 NIV

"Give, and it will be given to you. A good measure, pressed down, shaken together and running over, will be poured into your lap. For with the measure you use, it will be measured to you."
LUKE 6:38 NIV

GOD KEEPS HIS PROMISES

Know therefore that the LORD your God is God;
he is the faithful God, keeping his covenant of
love to a thousand generations of those who
love him and keep his commandments.

DEUTERONOMY 7:9 NIV

Human beings are untrustworthy, aren't they? If only folks would carry through on commitment. Your friend says she will meet you for lunch on Tuesday, then cancels at the last minute. Your husband promises a vacation next summer, then schedules a business trip instead. We are let down, time after time, and this is especially painful when it happens with someone we're close to.

When others around you are letting you down, there is One who is always true to His Word. If He says it, He will do it. God won't ever let you down. His promises are "Yes!" and "Amen!" The Lord keeps His covenant (agreement) with you. What covenant is that? The one where He agrees never to leave or forsake you. The one that ends with the ultimate happily ever after. Now, that's a promise you can take to the bank. He says it and He will do it.

"Every word of God is flawless;
he is a shield to those who take refuge in him."

PROVERBS 30:5 NIV

For the word of the LORD
is right and true; he is faithful in all he does.

PSALM 33:4 NIV

Sanctify them by the truth;
your word is truth.

JOHN 17:17 NIV

WHEN WE SEEK GOD FIRST, HE COVERS OUR NEEDS

And do not set your heart on what you will eat or drink;
do not worry about it. For the pagan world runs after all
such things, and your Father knows that you need them.
But seek his kingdom, and these things
will be given to you as well.
LUKE 12:29–31 NIV

What do you seek first? It's an interesting question, right? Some seek advancement at work. Others seek riches or fame. Still others seek a family—a spouse, children, or other loved ones. There's nothing wrong with longing for these things. However, the original question remains: What do you seek *first*? What's the very first thing you wish you had?

The Bible gives us an amazing promise: If we seek God first, then He will graciously provide all that we need. Puts things in perspective, right? When we remember this, we don't have to fret about anything—our provision, our strength, *anything*. Let others chase after these things. You don't need to do so. God has everything you need in the palm of His mighty hand.

Glory in his holy name; let the hearts
*of those who seek the L*ORD *rejoice.*
1 CHRONICLES 16:10 NIV

*Look to the L*ORD *and his strength;*
seek his face always.
1 CHRONICLES 16:11 NIV

And without faith it is impossible to please
God, because anyone who comes to him must
believe that he exists and that he rewards
those who earnestly seek him.
HEBREWS 11:6 NIV

I CAN MOVE FORWARD

Brothers and sisters, I know that I have not yet
reached that goal, but there is one thing I always
do. Forgetting the past and straining toward what is
ahead, I keep trying to reach the goal and get the prize
for which God called me through Christ to the life above.

PHILIPPIANS 3:13–14 NCV

Picture yourself stuck in quicksand, unable to move forward or backward. Not a very pleasant feeling, is it? That "stuck" feeling is miserable, especially when you have a desire to be in a different (better) place.

There's good news today! You can press toward the goal, even if you feel stuck. God's Word promises that you have the capability of reaching forward to what lies ahead, no matter where you are right now. If your feet are in quicksand (i.e., you're in a situation where you feel stuck) don't focus on your feet. Look up. Look ahead. Strain forward, even if it requires extreme levels of courage and strength. Lean your body in a forward position and watch as God propels you out of a "stuck"

place into a new one, far beyond anything you antici-
pated. Put the past behind you once and for all. God is
calling you to newer, bigger things.

Then Jesus told his disciples a parable
to show them that they should always
pray and not give up.

LUKE 18:1 NIV

Since we live by the Spirit,
let us keep in step with the Spirit.

GALATIANS 5:25 NIV

Therefore let us move beyond the elementary
teachings about Christ and be taken forward to
maturity, not laying again the foundation of repentance
from acts that lead to death, and of faith in God.

HEBREWS 6:1 NIV

I CAN BRING GOD PLEASURE

For it is God who is at work in you,
both to will and to work for His good pleasure.

PHILIPPIANS 2:13 NASB

Little girls love to entertain their families with silly songs, dances, and stories. They live to bring pleasure to those who will watch them. Perhaps you have a memory of "putting on a show" for your parents or singing a goofy song you'd created. Their applause brought you such joy and invigorated you.

When our children entertain us, we capture the moments on video or in photos and share the experience with others because we're so tickled. Did you realize that God is just as tickled with us? It's true! It's His good pleasure working inside of us. No, we're not putting on a show for Him, but every time we bless others—feed the poor, care for the sick, take care of our families, worship at His footstool, spend time with a loved one who's in pain—God is delighted. How wonderful to know that we can bring our Abba such pleasure!

*The godly people in the land
are my true heroes!
I take pleasure in them!*

PSALM 16:3 NLT

*For the LORD takes pleasure
in His people; He will beautify
the humble with salvation.*

PSALM 149:4 NKJV

*May the glory of the LORD continue
forever! The LORD takes pleasure
in all he has made!*

PSALM 104:31 NLT

GOD WILL DELIVER US

And the Lord shall help them and deliver them;
He shall deliver them from the wicked,
and save them, because they trust in Him.

PSALM 37:40 NKJV

As women, we understand the word *delivery*. We're "delivered" of our children as they exit our bodies and enter the world. In that moment, our literal ties to them are broken. We experience something akin to this when God "delivers" us from evil. We are (literally and symbolically) transported to a new place, all ties to darkness broken in an instant. We are, for the first time, breathing without the aid of our former sinful ties. What a revelation!

The Lord isn't just about delivering us from sin. He also longs to deliver us from selfishness, pain, and a variety of other things that hold us back. He's in the "delivery" business for sure! So, what's required on our end? One thing: trust. When we place our trust in the Lord, we set ourselves up for freedom.

*"And blessed be God Most High,
who has delivered your enemies into your
hand." And he gave him a tithe of all.*

GENESIS 14:20 NKJV

*For I know that as you pray for me and
the Spirit of Jesus Christ helps me,
this will lead to my deliverance.*

PHILIPPIANS 1:19 NLT

*God is to us a God of deliverances;
and to GOD the Lord belong
escapes from death.*

PSALM 68:20 NASB

WE CAN BE CONTENT IN HIM

Now godliness with
contentment is great gain.
1 Timothy 6:6 NKJV

To be content means you've settled an issue in your heart and don't spend your days wishing and hoping for things you don't have. Sure, you have longings and desires, but they don't drive you or force you to feel like you're somehow missing out on "the good life."

No matter your financial or relational situation, God has already given you the best possible life through His Son. Sure, your bank account might not be full. Your house might not be the finest in the neighborhood. Your clothes probably don't qualify you for the best-dressed list. But you're still rich. Eternal life is yours, bought and paid for by the King of kings and Lord of lords! And check it out! One day you will live in a mansion and walk on streets of gold. Wow! In the meantime, godly contentment will go a long way in preparing you for the bliss you will one day experience beyond heaven's pearly gates.

If they obey and serve him, they will spend
the rest of their days in prosperity
and their years in contentment.

JOB 36:11 NIV

I am not saying this because I am in need,
for I have learned to be content
whatever the circumstances.

PHILIPPIANS 4:11 NIV

Keep your lives free from the love
of money and be content with what
you have, because God has
said, "Never will I leave you;
never will I forsake you."

HEBREWS 13:5 NIV

GOD WILL TURN YOU INTO A SINGER!

*He put a new song in my mouth, a song of praise
to our God. Many people will see this and
worship him. Then they will trust the LORD.*

PSALM 40:3 NCV

Do you love to sing? Wish you knew how? Don't fret. God promises to put a song in your mouth, and not just any song! He wants this joyous chorus to bubble up inside of you so that many will hear it and trust God, just like you do!

Maybe you argue with this idea, claiming, "I'm not a good singer! I can't let anyone hear this voice of mine." (Maybe you're even cringing as you read this!) The Bible doesn't say we have to be good singers to praise the Lord; it simply says that we should "make a joyful noise" to Him. Anyone is capable of obedience.

So, put aside your fears related to your singing abilities and join in the song of praise. You're going to be singing for all eternity, after all! Might as well start warming up that voice right now.

Praise the LORD, because he is good;
sing praises to him, because it is pleasant.

PSALM 135:3 NCV

I will praise the LORD all my life;
I will sing praises to my God as long as I live.

PSALM 146:2 NCV

The LORD is my strength and my shield; my heart trusts in
him, and he helps me. My heart leaps for joy,
and with my song I praise him.

PSALM 28:7 NIV

HE SUPPLIES OUR NEEDS

And my God will meet all your
needs according to the riches of
his glory in Christ Jesus.
PHILIPPIANS 4:19 NIV

Imagine you worked for a grocery store. Every night the trucks would arrive from all over the country with the supplies you needed to stock your shelves. Without their delivery, you would run out of products to sell in a hurry. Customers would still show up at your door, but you would need to turn them away.

Aren't you glad that God is your ultimate supplier? When you're feeling depleted and when you don't think there's anything inside of you left to give, He supplies you with strength, courage, tenacity, and favor. He won't fail you. You won't be getting a "Sorry, I can't make it today" call from the Lord. God will always come through as your supplier.

It's not up to you. You don't have the supply. He does. You're the conduit through which He flows. And you will never run dry. That's a promise you can take to the bank.

"You will drink from the brook,
and I have directed the ravens to
supply you with food there."
1 KINGS 17:4 NIV

Now he who supplies seed to the sower
and bread for food will also supply and
increase your store of seed and will enlarge
the harvest of your righteousness.
2 CORINTHIANS 9:10 NIV

So Abraham named that place The LORD
Provides. Even today people say, "On the
mountain of the LORD it will be provided."
GENESIS 22:14 NCV

PATIENCE PAYS OFF

*I waited patiently for the LORD; and He inclined to
me and heard my cry. He brought me up out of the pit
of destruction, out of the miry clay, and He set my feet
upon a rock making my footsteps firm. He put a new
song in my mouth, a song of praise to our God;
many will see and fear and will trust in the LORD.*

PSALM 40:1–3 NASB

Have you ever felt as if God kept you waiting? Maybe
you wondered if He would ever show up. Then, miraculously, He came through at the eleventh hour. What
a relief!

Waiting is painful, particularly if we're in a tough
situation. We pace. We fume. We grumble. Rarely do
we sit quietly, hearts filled with joy as we wait it out.
Here's the good news: God rewards those who are diligent. The waiting pays off. Today's scripture proves the
point. When the Lord shows up in a situation, He lifts
you out of the miry clay (the pit) and places your feet
on a rock. Now that's worth waiting on!

If you're in a "waiting" season, don't give up. God hears your cries. He really does. And He's going to come through in a big way. In the meantime, try praising instead of grumbling. It makes the wait so much sweeter.

The end of a matter is better than its beginning;
patience of spirit is better than haughtiness of spirit.
ECCLESIASTES 7:8 NASB

And the seed that fell on the good ground is like those
who hear God's teaching with good, honest hearts
and obey it and patiently produce good fruit.
LUKE 8:15 NCV

But the fruit of the Spirit is love, joy, peace, patience,
kindness, goodness, faithfulness.
GALATIANS 5:22 NASB

SOLID AS A ROCK

Yes, my soul, find rest in God; my hope comes
from him. Truly he is my rock and my salvation;
he is my fortress, I will not be shaken.

PSALM 62:5–6 NIV

If you've ever been through an earthquake, you know the power of a good shaking. In that moment, you are more vulnerable than ever. Around you, life is crumbling—literally. It's hard to know what to hold on to. Everything seems vulnerable to the motion coming from below.

Now picture yourself going through a spiritual or emotional earthquake. Your world, as you know it, is shaken. You wonder if you will survive it.

What if you grabbed hold of the promise in this verse? What if you truly believed that life's shakings wouldn't affect you from the inside out? Would it change anything? God is your rock. That means He's the safest thing to grab on to. He's your fortress and when you take hold of His hand, you won't be shaken. What an amazing promise!

The LORD is my rock and my fortress and my deliverer,
my God, my rock, in whom I take refuge; my shield
and the horn of my salvation, my stronghold.

PSALM 18:2 NASB

The LORD lives! May my Rock be praised.
Praise the God who saves me!

PSALM 18:46 NCV

For who is God, but the LORD?
And who is a rock, except our God.

PSALM 18:31 NASB

RIGHTEOUS LIVING BLESSES MY CHILDREN

The righteous lead blameless lives;
blessed are their children after them.
PROVERBS 20:7 NIV

Want to know the best possible way to bless your kids and grandkids? Live a righteous life. It's not just a matter of those kids watching and mimicking you; there's more to it than that. When you live a righteous life, God is watching. And blessing. You are leaving a very special legacy for your children and grandchildren, and this makes Him happy. He, in turn, bestows blessing upon blessing.

If you're struggling with sin in your life, it's not just important to overcome it for your own sake, but the sake of your offspring as well. Let the "family blessing" begin with you. Righteous living will turn things around for the whole family. The legacy will be remarkable, and it can all start with you. What a fun promise!

*Through these he gave us the very great and precious
promises. With these gifts you can share in God's nature,
and the world will not ruin you with its evil desires.*

2 PETER 1:4 NCV

*The righteous man will be glad in
the LORD and will take refuge in Him;
and all the upright in heart will glory.*

PSALM 64:10 NASB

*The righteous man will flourish like
the palm tree, he will grow like
a cedar in Lebanon.*

PSALM 92:12 NASB

GOD FORGETS OUR SINS

*"For I will forgive their wickedness
and will remember their sins no more."*

HEBREWS 8:12 NIV

It boggles the mind to think that God might be willing to not only forgive our sins, but *forget* them as well. How can God, the all-knowing, possibly forget? And yet, He promises to do so.

If only we could forget when we forgive others for the things they've done to wound us. What a blissful situation, to have no recollection of the past wrongs done to us.

So, how does God forget? He chooses to do it. That's pretty much the same strategy we have to use when "choosing" to turn away from sin. It's a deliberate effort on our part. And notice, today's scripture doesn't say "sin." The word is "sins" (plural). We're tempted on every front. There's much to overcome, but we have this proof that overcoming all sinful behavior really is possible.

Praise the Lord! We can overcome, and God chooses to forget! Now, that's a "win-win over sin" situation!

Therefore, if anyone is in Christ,
the new creation has come:
The old has gone, the new is here!
2 CORINTHIANS 5:17 NIV

"I, even I, am he who blots out your
transgressions, for my own sake,
and remembers your sins no more."
ISAIAH 43:25 NIV

Hide your face from my sins
and blot out all my iniquity.
PSALM 51:9 NIV

WE HAVE A SUPPLIER

And my God shall supply all your need
according to His riches in glory by Christ Jesus.

PHILIPPIANS 4:19 NKJV

Wouldn't it be wonderful to shop at a store that didn't require payment? Imagine taking all of your purchases to the register, only to hear the words, "No money required!" from the clerk. What a lovely surprise.

In a sense, we can hear those same words from the Lord every day if we're listening closely. His salvation—eternal life—came to us free of charge. The cost was on His end. And in that same way, God supplies all of our needs on a daily basis. He's the one making provision, whether we acknowledge it or not. Your job? He arranged all that! The lower price on your car? He was behind that too. Your paycheck? Sure, it comes with your employer's name on it, but your real source is the Lord.

God promises to meet your needs. That means you don't have to fret over where the next meal or clothing is coming from. He's got it covered—in His time and

His own unique way. So, no worries. God, who owns the cattle on a thousand hills, can certainly meet your needs.

Now he who supplies seed to the sower and bread for food will also supply and increase your store of seed and will enlarge the harvest of your righteousness.

2 CORINTHIANS 9:10 NIV

Our Lord Jesus is the great Shepherd of the sheep. The God who gives peace brought him back from the dead. He did it because of the blood of the eternal covenant. Now may God supply you with everything good. Then you can do what he wants. May he do in us what is pleasing to him. We can do it only with the help of Jesus Christ.

HEBREWS 13:20–21 NIRV

Our storerooms will be filled with every kind of food. The sheep in our fields will increase by thousands.

PSALM 144:13 NIRV

I'M A HOLY HOUSE

*You also, like living stones, are being
built into a spiritual house to be a holy
priesthood, offering spiritual sacrifices
acceptable to God through Jesus Christ.*

1 PETER 2:5 NIV

If you could design your dream house, what would it look like? What would transpire inside of that house once built? It's fun to dream, isn't it?

Did you know that you are being built into a spiritual house? It's true. Today's scripture makes it clear that believers are "living" stones being built up into a spiritual house. Pause to think about that for a moment. You're a living stone. Not brick and mortar, the stuff used to build an ordinary abode. You're alive in Him, and not just while you're on earth either. You're alive for all eternity.

The "dwelling" that He's building is a forever kind of house. Termites won't tear it down. Wind and rain won't blow it over. It will stand the test of time. What is the purpose of this house? To offer up praises to the Lord. Your very life is a praise offering. Talk about a heavenly home!

Blessed are those you choose and bring
near to live in your courts! We are filled with the
good things of your house, of your holy temple.

PSALM 65:4 NIV

I will bow down toward your holy temple and will praise
your name for your unfailing love and your faithfulness,
for you have so exalted your solemn decree
that it surpasses your fame.

PSALM 138:2 NIV

But I, by your great love, can come into your house;
in reverence I bow down toward your holy temple.

PSALM 5:7 NIV

WE HAVE NOTHING TO BE AFRAID OF

Even though I walk through the darkest valley,
I will fear no evil, for you are with me;
your rod and your staff, they comfort me.

PSALM 23:4 NIV

What if you could speak to fear and watch it disappear? You would do it every time, wouldn't you? Here's a promise from God's Word: When we walk through dark and scary times, when we're really afraid, He promises to bring comfort. Yes, the valleys might be deep. You might feel swallowed up in shadows as you make your way along the unfamiliar terrain. But God has a way of shining His light into even the deepest of places, bringing peace and comfort.

When God shows up in a situation, fear disappears in an instant. Does that mean the "situation" instantly disappears? No. You have to keep walking, even when the road is rocky. But knowing the Lord is there with His arms around you will help so much. The journey through life's valleys is bearable when you're not alone.

What do you have to do to receive this comfort? Cry out to Him. Acknowledge your broken heart, your pain. He knows it all anyway. Then expect Him to pour His love and comfort over on you.

Peace I leave with you; my peace I give you. I do not give to you as the world gives. Do not let your hearts be troubled and do not be afraid.

JOHN 14:27 NIV

LORD, you will give perfect peace to those who commit themselves to be faithful to you. That's because they trust in you.

ISAIAH 26:3 NIRV

The God who gives peace will soon crush Satan under your feet. May the grace of our Lord Jesus be with you.

ROMANS 16:20 NIRV

GOD CAN MAKE
MY PATH STRAIGHT

O Lord, lead me in what is right and good,
because of the ones who hate me.
Make Your way straight in front of me.

PSALM 5:8 NLV

We live in the age of modern technology. When we need directions, we turn on our GPS or use the navigational app on our smartphone. Rarely do we lean on our "knower" (that still, small voice inside us). We've become so dependent on others, so trusting of their voice, their words. That's not always a good thing, especially when we're talking about a "spiritual road" instead of a physical one. When we face those roads, we need to reawaken the "knower" inside of us and listen closely, especially when we feel lost.

Life is filled with crooked places. Sometimes it's hard to know which way to go. And there are always those standing nearby, encouraging us to take the wrong path. They don't want us to succeed. That's why it's critical to ask for the Lord's directions at every turn. He alone knows the right path for this juncture in your life. Lean on His spiritual GPS at every turn and you won't go wrong.

Lead me in Your truth and teach me. For You are the God Who saves me. I wait for You all day long.

PSALM 25:5 NLV

Happy are those who hear the joyful call to worship, for they will walk in the light of your presence, LORD. They rejoice all day long in your wonderful reputation. They exult in your righteousness.

PSALM 89:15–16 NLT

For those who follow godly paths will rest in peace when they die.

ISAIAH 57:2 NLT

GOD WILL NEVER ABANDON ME

For the sake of his great name the LORD
will not reject his people, because the LORD
was pleased to make you his own.

1 SAMUEL 12:22 NIV

We are God's people. Think about that phrase for a moment. We're His. We belong to Him. If you're part of a large family, no doubt you have reunions. When we all gather together, there's hardly room to contain everyone. Talk about a party!

Imagine how big God's family is! And He's pleased to make us His own. Our ultimate "reunion" will take place in heaven, but the party can start right now! Every time we gather together and worship with fellow believers, we're joining in!

We're not strangers to God. We're "fellow citizens" with millions of others around the globe who all have one important thing in common: We love the Lord our God with all our heart, soul, mind, and strength. Wow, what a family!

*Consequently, you are no longer foreigners
and strangers, but fellow citizens with God's people
and also members of his household.*

EPHESIANS 2:19 NIV

*Greet all God's people in Christ Jesus.
The brothers and sisters who are
with me send greetings.*

PHILIPPIANS 4:21 NIV

*Therefore, as God's chosen people,
holy and dearly loved, clothe yourselves
with compassion, kindness, humility,
gentleness and patience.*

COLOSSIANS 3:12 NIV

NOTHING CAN SEPARATE ME FROM GOD'S LOVE

For I am convinced that neither death, nor life, nor angels, nor principalities, nor things present, nor things to come, nor powers, nor height, nor depth, nor any other created thing, will be able to separate us from the love of God, which is in Christ Jesus our Lord.

ROMANS 8:38–39 NASB

Have you ever been separated from someone you loved? Maybe one of you moved away to another part of the country. Perhaps you went through the agony of a divorce. Maybe your child grew up and went to college in another state, or married and moved away. Perhaps you're struggling with the loss of a loved one.

It's hard to be apart, isn't it? You go through a period of grieving, for sure, and wonder if you'll ever see each other again. This is only natural.

What a blessed privilege to realize that we'll never be separated from God. Even if we mess up royally, He won't abandon us. Today's scriptural promise should bring great peace. Nothing in the universe will cause God to leave us. What comfort!

But I am like an olive tree flourishing
in the house of God; I trust in God's
unfailing love for ever and ever.

PSALM 52:8 NIV

I will always sing about the LORD's love;
I will tell of his loyalty from now on.

PSALM 89:1 NCV

May the Lord lead your hearts into
God's love and Christ's patience.

2 THESSALONIANS 3:5 NCV

WE CAN BE RID OF ANXIETY

Casting all your anxiety on Him,
because He cares for you.
1 Peter 5:7 NASB

If you've ever been fishing, you know what it's like to cast your line into the water. This move requires preparation, aim, and a sense of release. The same is true when we cast our anxieties on the Lord. It's a deliberate move on our part. We make up our minds (prepare), place the fears and worries at His feet (aim), and then let go (release).

And the best part of all? God doesn't worry! It's not in His nature to fret, so when we release our cares to Him, He doesn't lose sleep over them like we do. Instead, He carries the weight as if it's nothing at all. So the next time you're tempted to fret, the next time anxiety grips your heart, remember this scriptural promise: God wants to carry it for you. Why? Because He cares for you of course!

And He said to His disciples, "For this reason I say to you,
do not worry about your life, as to what you will eat;
nor for your body, as to what you will put on."

LUKE 12:22 NASB

Anxiety weighs down the heart,
but a kind word cheers it up.

PROVERBS 12:25 NIV

And which of you by worrying can add
a single hour to his life's span?

LUKE 12:25 NASB

WE HAVE FULLNESS IN CHRIST

And in Christ you have been brought to fullness.
He is the head over every power and authority.

COLOSSIANS 2:10 NIV

You know that amazing feeling you have after Christmas dinner? You're full to the brim. Content. Ready to settle in for a long winter's nap. Ah, what bliss!

Did you know that you can sense that same type of fullness on a spiritual level when you spend time in God's presence? It's true. Even on days when you wake up feeling empty inside, the Lord can fill your tank—your spiritual tank—with His Spirit. He can take a "nothing" day and make it "something" in a hurry. So, what are you waiting for? If you're ready to experience His fullness, run into His arms today. When you do, His power and authority are yours. No lack! No void. You'll be filled to overflowing, ready for whatever tasks come your way.

*You will show me the path of life; in Your presence
is fullness of joy; at Your right hand are
pleasures forevermore.*

PSALM 16:11 NKJV

*To equip his people for works of service, so that the body
of Christ may be built up until we all reach unity
in the faith and in the knowledge of the Son of God
and become mature, attaining to the whole
measure of the fullness of Christ.*

EPHESIANS 4:12–13 NIV

*They are abundantly satisfied with the fullness
of Your house, and You give them drink
from the river of Your pleasures.*

PSALM 36:8 NKJV

I CAN STAND FIRM

*Finally, my brethren, be strong in the Lord and in
the power of His might. Put on the whole armor
of God, that you may be able to stand
against the wiles of the devil.*

EPHESIANS 6:10–11 NKJV

When you think of the words "stand firm" what comes to mind? Take a moment to picture yourself standing in front of a bully with his fists doubled up, ready to take you down. He's bigger than you are and has some buddies with him, ready to help him out, if necessary. Could you stand firm, even with that evil look in his eye?

The Bible promises that, when we're fully equipped with God's armor, we can stand firm, even under the toughest of circumstances. Even when life's "bullies" are taunting us.

We can do so without wavering, even in the middle of the battle. We might be tempted to turn on our heels and run, but God prompts us to hold our position. In doing so, we call the enemy's bluff. He tucks his tail between his legs and scampers off. So stand firm!

Give your way over to the Lord.
Trust in Him also. And He will do it.

PSALM 37:5 NLV

Teach me to do your will, for you
are my God. May your gracious Spirit
lead me forward on a firm footing.

PSALM 143:10 NLT

Therefore, put on every piece of God's
armor so you will be able to resist the
enemy in the time of evil. Then after the
battle you will still be standing firm.

EPHESIANS 6:13 NLT

SEAL THE DEAL

Now it is God who makes both us
and you stand firm in Christ. He anointed us,
set his seal of ownership on us, and put his Spirit in
our hearts as a deposit, guaranteeing what is to come.

2 CORINTHIANS 1:21–22 NIV

Imagine taking your leftovers (yum!) and putting them in a ziplock bag. You place them in the fridge, with plans to eat them tomorrow. Then "tomorrow" comes and you reach into the fridge, only to discover the bag wasn't properly sealed. The food has leaked out all over the place. Ick! What a mess!

To be "sealed" means there's no chance of destruction after-the-fact. When your food is properly sealed, it's perfectly good the next day, just as you left it. Think about that for a moment. When Jesus died on the cross, He "sealed the deal" for us. Nothing can "unseal" His eternal work on Calvary! He's even given us His Spirit as a pledge.

Nothing will change God's mind. We're His. And we don't need to fear "destruction" of any kind as long as we are sealed in Him. We are safe and secure, standing firm. He's even put His Spirit in our hearts as a deposit (promise) of what's to come.

"The Spirit of the Lord is upon me, because he has anointed me to proclaim good news to the poor. He has sent me to proclaim liberty to the captives and recovering of sight to the blind, to set at liberty those who are oppressed."

LUKE 4:18 ESV

"You love justice and hate evil. Therefore, O God, your God has anointed you, pouring out the oil of joy on you more than on anyone else."

HEBREWS 1:9 NLT

For sin will have no dominion over you, since you are not under law but under grace.

ROMANS 6:14 ESV

WHEN WE ARE IN HIM,
WE ARE NOT CONDEMNED

*Therefore, there is now no condemnation
for those who are in Christ Jesus.*

ROMANS 8:1 NIV

We can be so hard on ourselves, can't we? We look in the mirror and critique our appearance. We begin a task with vigor, then feel we fall short after-the-fact. We work all day, caring for kids, house, job, spouse, and still feel as if we don't have as much value as others.

Aren't you glad that God doesn't critique us in the same way? He's not standing over us, clucking His tongue and saying, "Can't you get *anything* right?" When we come to Him, accepting His gift of salvation, all the icky stuff (worthy of critique) is washed away. There's nothing left to comment on!

Sure, we still make mistakes. At times we will break His heart with our actions. But even then, God doesn't waggle His finger in our face, blasting us for what we've done. He gently woos us back with His amazing love then pours out grace and mercy. Condemnation is a thing of the past when we're walking with Him. Praise God for that!

For God did not send his Son into the world to condemn the world, but in order that the world might be saved through him.

JOHN 3:17 ESV

If we confess our sins, he is faithful and just and will forgive us our sins and purify us from all unrighteousness.

1 JOHN 1:9 NIV

"I, even I, am the One Who takes away your sins because of Who I am. And I will not remember your sins. Make Me remember, and let us talk together. Make your cause known, that you may be shown not to be guilty."

ISAIAH 43:25–26 NLV

ALL THINGS ARE MADE NEW

*Therefore, if anyone is in Christ, the new creation
has come: The old has gone, the new is here!*

2 CORINTHIANS 5:17 NIV

Picture a woman in her midnineties. Frail. Arthritic. Wrinkled. Now picture God breathing new life into her body and taking it back to the health and vitality of a woman in her twenties. What an amazing miracle, to be completely restored! Can you imagine?

That's what it's like when Christ breathes new life into us. The old, wrinkled self is whisked away in an instant, replaced with a new, life-filled one. Gone are the days of arthritic hobbling. Gone are the moments of foggy thinking. Gone are the fears of death. God recreates, making the old new again, turning death to life, making impossible possible. The "old" is made brand new, like a little child. (Can you picture the expression on the woman's face? How delightful!)

What are you hoping for today? Trust God, the "all things new Creator," to do the work inside of you. He's in the restoration business, after all, ready to turn back the clock and give you a second chance.

Since you have been born again,
not of perishable seed but of imperishable,
through the living and abiding word of God.

1 PETER 1:23 ESV

Of his own will he brought us forth by the
word of truth, that we should be a kind
of firstfruits of his creatures.

JAMES 1:18 ESV

I have been crucified with Christ. It is no
longer I who live, but Christ who lives in me.
And the life I now live in the flesh I live by faith
in the Son of God, who loved me
and gave himself for me.

GALATIANS 2:20 ESV

SAVED, NOT JUDGED

For God did not send his Son into the
world to condemn the world,
but to save the world through him.

JOHN 3:17 NIV

If you've ever testified in court, you've had ample opportunity to watch the judge at work. He's not just sitting there as an authority figure. He is a decision maker—the ultimate decision maker, in fact.

God is the Creator of all, and the only true "judge" whose opinion counts. He could slam down His gavel and proclaim our guilt, but He chooses another route. Instead, He looks at us, seated there in the chair across from Him, guilty and stained, and says, "My Son paid your debt; therefore, I commute your sentence. Walk in freedom." Wow! Jesus paid our debt and we've been declared innocent.

Take a close look at today's verse. Jesus didn't come to judge us. He came to save us. What thrilling news and what a precious promise.

*For by grace you have been saved through faith.
And this is not your own doing; it is the gift of God,
not a result of works, so that no one may boast.*

EPHESIANS 2:8–9 ESV

*And they said, "Believe in the Lord
Jesus, and you will be saved,
you and your household."*

ACTS 16:31 ESV

*Truly, truly, I say to you, whoever hears my word and
believes him who sent me has eternal life. He does not
come into judgment, but has passed from death to life.*

JOHN 5:24 ESV

GIVE AND IT WILL BE GIVEN

"Give, and it will be given to you. A good measure,
pressed down, shaken together and running over,
will be poured into your lap. For with the measure
you use, it will be measured to you."

LUKE 6:38 NIV

Are you a giver or a taker? It's an interesting question, isn't it? Most of us would consider ourselves givers. We give, give, give. But, if we examine our hearts, many of us find that we're really takers. We long for things we don't have. We're dissatisfied. We want more. We compare ourselves to others and struggle with bouts of jealousy.

Want to know how to overcome the "taker" attitude? Give more! That's right. Give even more. Giving turns our focus away from self and toward others. Before long, we see the plight of the one we're helping and it puts our selfish (or even unselfish) desires in perspective.

It's not wrong to want things. Unless those "things"— or the desire to have them—consume you. That's why this verse speaks to us in our time of "wanting," because

God promises to meet our needs when we give.
What are you waiting for? Get busy giving!

"In all things I have shown you that by working hard in
this way we must help the weak and remember the
words of the Lord Jesus, how he himself said,
'It is more blessed to give than to receive.'"
ACTS 20:35 ESV

Whoever is kind to the poor lends to the LORD,
and he will reward them for what they have done.
PROVERBS 19:17 NIV

Do not neglect to do good and to share what you
have, for such sacrifices are pleasing to God.
HEBREWS 13:16 ESV

WE HAVE A SHIELD

*As for God, his way is perfect: The LORD's word is
flawless; he shields all who take refuge in him.*

PSALM 18:30 NIV

Can you picture a warrior going off to battle with no
way to protect himself? Marching bravely in front of
the enemy without the proper shield would be foolish.
It's equally foolish to think that we can do battle against
the enemy of our souls without being properly equipped.
When we give our hearts to the Lord, He covers us.
We can take refuge under His wing. In essence, we are
shielded when we stick close to Him.

So many times we set out on our own, thinking,
"I've got this. Don't need any help, thanks!" We forget to
include God. When we do this, we come out from under
His safety net. It's better to hover safely under His wing.

Stick close, so that He can be your shield. Don't
have a "go it alone" attitude, or you will surely pay the
price! Why would you want to live in your own strength
when His Word promises that He will shield you?

But you, LORD, are a shield around me,
my glory, the One who lifts my head high.

PSALM 3:3 NIV

For You, O LORD, will bless the righteous;
with favor You will surround him
as with a shield.

PSALM 5:12 NKJV

I am kept safe by God, Who saves
those who are pure in heart.

PSALM 7:10 NLV

GOD CARES ABOUT OUR DESIRES

Be happy in the Lord. And He will
give you the desires of your heart.

PSALM 37:4 NLV

Think back to when you were a child. What did you dream of being when you grew up? What did you dream of doing? Where did you long to travel? Who did you hope to marry? What sort of children did you want to have?

You might look at those childish dreams now and think they're a thing of the past. Not so! God cares very much about the desires of your heart. He longs to see you giddy with delight over the blessings He can bestow.

If you really want to benefit from all that the Lord has in store, make up your mind to be content, no matter what. When you're "happy in the Lord" (as today's scripture suggests) He will give you the desires of your heart. If you walk around unhappy all the time, grumbling and complaining, those blessings might be a little slower in coming. So be happy! That's the way to live.

He fills my years with good things
and I am made young again like the eagle.

PSALM 103:5 NLV

He grants the desires of those who fear him;
he hears their cries for help and rescues them.

PSALM 145:19 NLT

Those who live according to the flesh
have their minds set on what the flesh desires;
but those who live in accordance with the Spirit
have their minds set on what the Spirit desires.

ROMANS 8:5 NIV

WHEN WE COME TO HIM, HE GIVES US REST

"Come to me, all you who are weary and burdened, and I will give you rest."

MATTHEW 11:28 NIV

What a crazy rush-about world we live in. Everything moves at lightning-fast speed. We zip, zip, zip from one thing to another, rarely pausing to breathe in between events. Whew! Rushing around is exhausting, and we pay a price with our health if we're not careful.

God never intended for us to be on the go 'round the clock. In fact, His Word is pretty clear that we're meant to take sabbaticals at least once a week. For some, a "season of rest" might be in order.

Think about your own life. Are you overdue for a break? If so, ask the Lord to show you how you can take Him up on this promise: that you can come to Him (weary and heavy-laden) and experience true rest and refreshment. He will do it! You simply have to take the time to meet Him there. Ah, rest! Doesn't that sound lovely?

*By the seventh day God had finished the work
he had been doing; so on the seventh
day he rested from all his work.*

GENESIS 2:2 NIV

*I said, "Oh, that I had the wings of a
dove! I would fly away and be at rest."*

PSALM 55:6 NIV

*He who dwells in the secret place of the Most High
shall abide under the shadow of the Almighty.*

PSALM 91:1 NKJV

*My people will dwell in a peaceful habitation,
in secure dwellings, and in quiet resting places.*

ISAIAH 32:18 NKJV

WHEN WE RECEIVE HIM, WE BECOME HIS KIDS

But as many as received Him, to them
He gave the right to become children of God,
to those who believe in His name.

JOHN 1:12 NKJV

Those of us who are grandparents know the joy of sweeping lots of little ones into the fold. They bring such delight! No, they weren't born to us, but they have snagged a piece of our heart and won't let go.

Imagine how God must feel when He gazes into the faces of billions of His kids. What joy it must bring our heavenly Father to dote on each of us, to care for our needs and to provide with unending riches. On the same hand, how difficult it must be to watch us squirm, or to live rebellious lives. Today's scriptural promise is amazing: We have a right to be children of God because we believe in His name. With that right comes a true responsibility—to make our Daddy proud, indeed!

Blessed are the peacemakers,
for they shall be called sons of God.

MATTHEW 5:9 NKJV

When Jesus saw this, he was indignant.
He said to them, "Let the little children
come to me, and do not hinder them, for the
kingdom of God belongs to such as these."

MARK 10:14 NIV

For those who are led by the Spirit
of God are the children of God.

ROMANS 8:14 NIV

So in Christ Jesus you are
all children of God through faith.

GALATIANS 3:26 NIV

IF I HUMBLE MYSELF, GOD WILL LIFT ME UP

For those who exalt themselves will be humbled,
and those who humble themselves will be exalted.

MATTHEW 23:12 NIV

Ah, humility! We talk about it, but living it is a completely different thing. No one sets out to be prideful, but it's so difficult not to put personal needs, personal desires, first. Still, when we humble ourselves and focus on others, God will lift us up. He does a far better job of exalting than we could ever do! We don't have to shine a spotlight on our faces to draw attention. He takes care of exalting what needs to be exalted.

Have you been guilty of bragging or drawing too much attention to yourself? Do you have a tendency to overshare the positive things in your life, even when others around you are hurting? Maybe it's time to trim back and let God shine His spotlight on you, if and when He desires. When you humble yourself (turn the spotlight off of "self"), God is free to shine at His finest!

If my people, who are called by my name, will humble themselves and pray and seek my face and turn from their wicked ways, then I will hear from heaven, and I will forgive their sin and will heal their land.

2 Chronicles 7:14 NIV

You save the humble but bring low those whose eyes are haughty.

Psalm 18:27 NIV

He leads those without pride into what is right, and teaches them His way.

Psalm 25:9 NLV

For the Lord is happy with His people. He saves those who have no pride and makes them beautiful.

Psalm 149:4 NLV

A LITTLE FAITH

He replied, "Because you have so little faith. Truly I tell
you, if you have faith as small as a mustard seed,
you can say to this mountain, 'Move from here to there,'
and it will move. Nothing will be impossible for you."

MATTHEW 17:20 NIV

Somewhere along the way, most of us got the wrong idea
about faith. We longed for—and hoped to achieve—
massive amounts of it. We wanted to topple evil king-
doms. Slay giants. Speak to mountains and watch them
crumble. And we felt sure that our puny version of faith
wouldn't be enough to do the trick.

How amazing, to learn that a teensy-tiny amount
of faith (as small as a grain of sand or a mustard seed)
is adequate to get the job done. We don't have to wait
around until our faith grows. We can start toppling
mountains right now.

Oh, ye of little faith! What are you waiting for? Put
that mustard seed into action and then watch it grow,
grow, grow!

Consequently, faith comes from hearing the message, and the message is heard through the word about Christ.

ROMANS 10:17 NIV

The goal of this command is love, which comes from a pure heart and a good conscience and a sincere faith.

1 TIMOTHY 1:5 NIV

Fight the good fight of the faith. Take hold of the eternal life to which you were called when you made your good confession in the presence of many witnesses.

1 TIMOTHY 6:12 NIV

CLOTHED IN PEACE

Let the peace of Christ rule in your
hearts, since as members of one body
you were called to peace. And be thankful.

COLOSSIANS 3:15 NIV

Today's scripture on peace is an interesting one, isn't it? When you think about something "ruling" over you, a king or government usually comes to mind. Perhaps a court of law. Rarely would you think of "peace" playing the role of ruler, but that's what today's scriptural promise suggests.

So, what does it mean to allow peace to "rule" our hearts? In order for that to take place, we have to submit ourselves to the process. We have to willingly approach God and say, "I can't live in chaos and turmoil any-more, Lord. I give up. Please replace my angst with Your peace." Then, after making that commitment, we must trust that God will flood our hearts with His unmistak-able peace every time we're tempted to get anxious. Can we live like this moment to moment? If we trust Him, yes. What an amazing promise!

Do not be anxious about anything, but in every situation,
by prayer and petition, with thanksgiving, present
your requests to God. And the peace of God,
which transcends all understanding, will guard
your hearts and your minds in Christ Jesus.

PHILIPPIANS 4:6–7 NIV

Now, brothers and sisters, I say good-bye. Live in
harmony. Do what I have asked you to do. Agree with
each
other, and live in peace. Then the God
of love and peace will be with you.

2 CORINTHIANS 13:11 NCV

But the Spirit produces the fruit of love, joy, peace,
patience, kindness, goodness, faithfulness.

GALATIANS 5:22 NCV

I CAN OVERCOME EVIL WITH GOOD

Do not let sin have power over you.
Let good have power over sin!
ROMANS 12:21 NLV

Most of us who love the Lord would argue that we are rarely "overcome" by sin and evil. However, there are days when our temper gets the best of us or depression sets in. We get overwhelmed. We might think this has nothing to do with "evil," but think again! Our enemy catches us off guard with cleverly disguised smoke and mirrors, doing all he can to distract us and pull us off course. We need to be aware of his tactics and be prepared to fight him at every turn.

We can overcome "evil" (his fiery darts) with good, but to do so we have to keep our eyes open. Maybe this is half the problem: we don't want to keep our eyes open because we're afraid of what we might see. We're scared.

Time to garner the courage to look sin in the eye and call it what it is. Only then can you overcome its grip on you. Once you release your hold, you're in a position to truly have power over sin for good.

"Will not your face be happy if you do well?
If you do not do well, sin is waiting to destroy you.
Its desire is to rule over you, but you must rule over it."

GENESIS 4:7 NLV

Tremble, and do not sin; Meditate in your
heart upon your bed, and be still. Selah.

PSALM 4:4 NASB

I acknowledged my sin to You, and my iniquity I did
not hide; I said, "I will confess my transgressions to
the LORD"; and You forgave the guilt of my sin. Selah.

PSALM 32:5 NASB

WE'RE ACCEPTED BY GOD

Accept one another, then, just as Christ
accepted you, in order to bring praise to God.

ROMANS 15:7 NIV

If you've ever "accepted" a package from a deliveryman, you know that "taking possession" is involved. You take it into your arms, your home, and your life. It becomes yours. The same is true when God accepts us into His kingdom. We become His. No longer outcasts, we are part of the family.

To be accepted means you don't have to work to earn God's love. What a relief! There's nothing we can do to be "un-accepted" either. God won't reject us if we make mistakes. This is why God is so keen on us accepting one another (fellow believers) in love. No judging. No divisions. *Just acceptance.* No, we don't all worship exactly the same way, but we serve the same heavenly Father and He longs for us to dwell together in unity. So, accept His love, and then accept your fellow believers as part of the family. In this way, you will show the Father's heart.

God, who knows the heart, showed that he accepted
them by giving the Holy Spirit to them, just as he did to us.

ACTS 15:8 NIV

People everywhere are telling about the way you
accepted us when we were there with you. They tell
how you stopped worshiping idols and began
serving the living and true God.

1 THESSALONIANS 1:9 NCV

"If you do what is right, will you not be accepted?
But if you do not do what is right, sin is crouching
at your door; it desires to have you,
but you must rule over it."

GENESIS 4:7 NIV

GOD GIVES YOU STRENGTH

The LORD gives strength to his people;
the LORD blesses his people with peace.

PSALM 29:11 NCV

Aren't you glad to hear that God gives us strength? It doesn't come from taking your vitamins. It doesn't come from working out (though both of those things probably help with physical strength). God-breathed strength is the sort that invigorates us even on days when we feel we can't put one foot in front of the other. It's an inside-out strength.

Are you needing some of this supernatural strength today? If so, acknowledge your need to your heavenly Father. Admitting your weakness is nothing to be ashamed of. In fact, admitting you can't handle something is a good thing because it frees God up to handle it for you. (Seriously. . .why would He intervene if you went around announcing that you had it all together?) So, admit you need help, then watch as He swoops in and gives you the strength to handle all you're facing.

The Lord says, "So I will teach those who make idols. This time I will teach them about my power and my strength. Then they will know that my name is the Lord."

JEREMIAH 16:21 NCV

All the angels were standing around the throne and around the elders and the four living creatures. They fell down on their faces before the throne and worshiped God, saying: "Amen! Praise and glory and wisdom and thanks and honor and power and strength be to our God for ever and ever. Amen!"

REVELATION 7:11–12 NIV

In your unfailing love you will lead the people you have redeemed. In your strength you will guide them to your holy dwelling.

EXODUS 15:13 NIV

BLESSED TO ENTER THE LAND

*See, I set before you today life and prosperity, death
and destruction. For I command you today to love the
Lord your God, to walk in obedience to him, and to keep
his commands, decrees and laws; then you will live
and increase, and the Lord your God will bless
you in the land you are entering to possess.*

DEUTERONOMY 30:15–16 NIV

God led the way for the Israelites to enter the Promised
Land, though it took a lot longer than expected. Maybe
you can relate to their situation. You've been waiting a
long time to enter your "promised land." Maybe you're
waiting on a spouse. Or a job. Or a child.

Perhaps you're longing for a lasting friendship or a
new, working vehicle. Whatever you're waiting on, rest
assured, God cares. He has blessed you to enter your
"promised land" but the timing of that entrance is completely up to Him. He sets choices in front of you. Some
are plain; others, not so much. When you walk in com-
munion with Him, it's easier to get His perspective when
you're facing several options. In the meantime, you are to

live according to His commands and decrees. When you do that, you will not only possess the land (according to His timetable) but be blessed along the way.

Do what is right and good in the LORD's sight,
so that it may go well with you and you may go
in and take over the good land the LORD
promised on oath to your ancestors.
DEUTERONOMY 6:18 NIV

"May he give you and your descendants the blessing
given to Abraham, so that you may take possession
of the land where you now reside as a foreigner,
the land God gave to Abraham."
GENESIS 28:4 NIV

I will surely bless you and make your descendants as
numerous as the stars in the sky and as the sand on the
seashore. Your descendants will take possession
of the cities of their enemies.
GENESIS 22:17 NIV

PROTECTED FROM THE EVIL ONE

But the Lord is faithful,
and he will strengthen you and
protect you from the evil one.

2 THESSALONIANS 3:3 NIV

Sometimes we forget that we have a very real enemy out there who wants to steal, kill, and destroy. We get so busy, so distracted, that we often don't see his tactics until we've been hit hard. Then, often, we don't have the energy or the wherewithal to fight.

It's during times like these that we can breathe a huge sigh of relief, not because we're okay with being attacked, but because we have an Advocate and Protector. God Himself protects us from the evil one. He intervenes, ready to take on the enemy full-force. He is our defense.

And watching all of this transpire does something to us. It energizes us for the next go-round with the enemy. Whenever he sneaks up on us once again, we're ready for him. We're strong from the inside-out because we know our Protector is nearby. How wonderful, the promise of safety!

Don't you realize that I could ask my
Father for thousands of angels to protect
us, and he would send them instantly?
MATTHEW 26:53 NLT

May the LORD answer you when you are in distress;
may the name of the God of Jacob protect you.
PSALM 20:1 NIV

May he reign under God's protection forever.
May your unfailing love and faithfulness watch over him.
PSALM 61:7 NLT

WE CAN BE REFRESHED

So you must change your hearts and lives!
Come back to God, and he will forgive your sins.
Then the Lord will send the time of rest.

ACTS 3:19 NCV

Picture yourself driving the wrong direction down a one-way street. Talk about treacherous! You finally realize the error of your ways and turn the car around. Whew! Now you can drive in complete safety.

That's a pretty clear picture of what it's like when we come to the Lord. We've been traveling in the wrong direction. Then we come face–to–face with God, through the person of His Son, and do a quick 180-degree turn. When we repent and make that turn, it's not just a matter of saying, "Thank You, Lord, for saving me so that I can one day go to heaven," it's more involved than that. We "turn" and seasons of refreshing come now. We don't have to wait for heaven. What glorious news!

"You should work six days a week, but on the seventh day you must rest. This lets your ox and your donkey rest, and it also lets the slave born in your house and the foreigner be refreshed."

EXODUS 23:12 NCV

"For I satisfy the weary ones and refresh everyone who languishes."

JEREMIAH 31:25 NASB

Yes, brother, let me benefit from you in the Lord; refresh my heart in Christ.

PHILEMON 1:20 NASB

GROWING AND GROWING

Yet he did not waver through unbelief regarding the
promise of God, but was strengthened in his faith and
gave glory to God, being fully persuaded that
God had power to do what he had promised.

ROMANS 4:20–21 NIV

Watching children grow up is so fascinating. One minute they're teensy-tiny, sipping on a baby bottle, the next they're toddling across the room. Before you know it, they're headed out the door for the first day of kindergarten, and not much later (in the grand scheme of things) they're walking down the aisle to get married. Time seems to fly!

In much the same way that our children grow, we can grow as believers. Our spiritual growth depends on our time in the Word and in prayer, but how fun to think that we're growing, growing, growing daily. How tickled God must be when He looks at the changes going on in our hearts and lives.

As we grow, we have to remain steady, unmoved by the various changes we're going through. When we do this, we will be strengthened in our faith and more convinced than ever that God will do amazing things in and through us.

We have come to share in Christ, if indeed we hold our original conviction firmly to the very end.

HEBREWS 3:14 NIV

In the same way, the gospel is bearing fruit and growing throughout the whole world—just as it has been doing among you since the day you heard it and truly understood God's grace.

COLOSSIANS 1:6 NIV

For this reason, since the day we heard about you, we have not stopped praying for you. We continually ask God to fill you with the knowledge of his will through all the wisdom and understanding that the Spirit gives, so that you may live a life worthy of the Lord and please him in every way: bearing fruit in every good work, growing in the knowledge of God.

COLOSSIANS 1:9-10 NIV

FEAR, BE GONE!

I sought the Lord, and He answered me,
and He delivered me from all my fears.

Psalm 34:4 nasb

Don't you wish you could look your fear in the face then holler, "Be gone! Get out of here! I don't want you hanging around anymore!"

Truth is, you can do all of that! Fear is a tool of the enemy and we can definitely send it packing. The key? We have to be willing to acknowledge it and bravely face it. This sounds easy, but in the moment (when faced with crippling terror) it is much harder than you thought it would be.

One way to get over this fear is to remember that God is the One fighting the battles for you. He's ultimately the one taking control. Still, He expects your participation! So, square those shoulders. Take a deep breath. Look your fears directly in the eye and let out a rip-roarin' "Get out of here!" at the top of your lungs. Then watch that fear skedaddle!

There is no fear in love; but perfect love casts out fear,
because fear involves punishment, and the
one who fears is not perfected in love.

1 John 4:18 NASB

Yes, my dear children, live in him so that when Christ
comes back, we can be without fear and
not be ashamed in his presence.

1 John 2:28 NCV

David also said to his son Solomon, "Be strong and
brave, and do the work. Don't be afraid or discouraged,
because the Lord God, my God, is with you.
He will not fail you or leave you until all the
work for the Temple of the Lord is finished."

1 Chronicles 28:20 NCV

I'M STRONGER THAN I KNOW

I can do all this through him
who gives me strength.

PHILIPPIANS 4:13 NIV

It's funny, if you think about it. Women are considered to be "the weaker sex" and yet they're the ones juggling jobs, kids, house, relationships, and often much more. There's nothing weak about it, especially if we're rooted in Christ. His strength rises up on the inside of us and invigorates us for the daily tasks we face. Sure, we still feel weak at times. Our bodies—and hearts—need ongoing periods of rest. But when we consider the fact that strength isn't something we muster up, when we bow to the idea that God's strength is enough to handle whatever we're facing, relief floods our souls.

You can do all things through Christ who strengthens you. Maybe you needed to hear that again today. *You* can because *He* can. And He will. Just ask, and then watch Him step in and give you the necessary strength to face whatever lies in front of you.

My flesh and my heart may fail,
but God is the strength of my heart
and my portion forever.

PSALM 73:26 NIV

No! In all these things we are more than winners!
We owe it all to Christ, who has loved us.

ROMANS 8:37 NIRV

She gets ready to work hard.
Her arms are strong.

PROVERBS 31:17 NIRV

HUMBLED LIKE A CHILD

Therefore, whoever takes the lowly position of
this child is the greatest in the kingdom of heaven.

MATTHEW 18:4 NIV

If you've ever watched a small child at play, you know that he's totally dependent on his elders. He's not bragging about how great he is or bossing the grown-ups around. He's submitted to the authority in his life, in part because he recognizes that everything he has comes from those who care about him.

Oh, if only we would come to God with that same sort of attitude. If only we could remember that everything we are, everything we will ever be, is because of His mercy and grace! That sort of humility is pleasing to the Lord. He's not keen on hearing us brag about how we've "made something of our lives" or "moved up the corporate ladder." Sure, we've played a role in those things, but ultimately the glory, and the credit, goes to Him. His love has propelled our growth and is at the core of all we do.

It's time to stop taking credit. We must acknowledge that He's the One in charge of it all. When we do that, He propels us to where we need to go. That's a promise!

So Moses and Aaron went to Pharaoh and said to him,
"This is what the LORD, the God of the Hebrews, says:
'How long will you refuse to humble yourself before me?
Let my people go, so that they may worship me.' "
EXODUS 10:3 NIV

Humble yourself in the Lord's
presence, and he will honor you.
JAMES 4:10 NCV

"Because your heart was tender and you humbled
yourself before God when you heard His words against
this place and against its inhabitants, and because you
humbled yourself before Me, tore your clothes and wept
before Me, I truly have heard you," declares the LORD.
2 CHRONICLES 34:27 NASB

A FOREVER GIFT

God never changes his mind about the
people he calls and the things he gives them.

ROMANS 11:29 NCV

Picture this: It's Christmas morning. You've just unwrapped a present that makes your heart sing. You carry it with you wherever you go. At first. After awhile you use it less and less. Eventually the person who gave you the gift says, "Hey, if you're not going to use that, I'm just going to take it back." You're shocked, but give it back.

Aren't you glad God isn't like that? When He gives you gifts (spiritual gifts/talents/abilities) He won't take them back. When you actively use those gifts, He's so pleased! And when you're in a sabbatical season—the gifts lie dormant—He hasn't given up on you. It's just a season.

So, hang in there. The gifts that God has placed inside of you are a blessing to you and to the body of Christ. And the Lord knew exactly who He could trust with them—you!

So it is with you. Since you are eager
for gifts of the Spirit, try to excel in
those that build up the church.
1 CORINTHIANS 14:12 NIV

If you then, being evil, know how to give good gifts
to your children, how much more will your Father who
is in heaven give good things to those who ask Him!
MATTHEW 7:11 NKJV

Now eagerly desire the greater gifts.
And yet I will show you the most excellent way.
1 CORINTHIANS 12:31 NIV

OUR ENEMIES WILL BE CLOTHED IN SHAME

"Those who hate you will be clothed with shame, and the dwelling place of the wicked will come to nothing."

JOB 8:22 NKJV

Have you ever been to a really formal event where everyone showed up in their finest? Then, through the door walked one random person wearing jeans and a T-shirt? Talk about standing out (and not in a good way).

Today's verse puts us in mind of a situation like that. Those who love the Lord are "dressed" in His finest (joy, peace, strength, and so on). According to this verse, those who oppose God's ways will be clothed in shame. Will their "literal" clothes make them seem out of place? Probably not. But they will wear shame like a cloak. It hangs over them, setting them apart.

So, don't fret when opposition comes from hardhearted people. God has His own way of taking care of those who shame His Word. Just keep wearing His clothing—mercy, grace, joy—and let Him deal with the wardrobe of others you meet along the way.

I put on righteousness, and it clothed me;
my justice was like a robe and a turban.

JOB 29:14 NKJV

Let my accusers be clothed with shame,
and let them cover themselves with their
own disgrace as with a mantle.

PSALM 109:29 NKJV

"Now arise, LORD God, and come to your
resting place, you and the ark of your
might. May your priests, LORD God,
be clothed with salvation, may your faithful
people rejoice in your goodness."

2 CHRONICLES 6:41 NIV

WE CAN LIVE FOREVER

*"Most assuredly, I say to you, he who hears My
word and believes in Him who sent Me has everlasting
life, and shall not come into judgment,
but has passed from death into life."*

John 5:24 NKJV

Have you ever contemplated the word *forever*? It's the
kind of word that leaves your head spinning. Sure, you
can read those "happily ever after" books and wonder
about our limited view of forever, but God's version of
forever goes on forever! Into eternity. Beyond the limita-
tions of our calendar.

Our finite minds can't comprehend eternity, but we
do get glimpses of it in God's Word. Eternal life isn't a
day-in, day-out drudgery. Heaven is going to be blissful.
And here's some happy news: Eternity has already begun
in your life if you've accepted Jesus as Lord of your life.
Your starting point kicked off the moment you said, "I
do!" to your Savior. So, you're already walking out your
eternity, and the bliss of that experience has begun.

Don't wait till you get to heaven to start celebrating either. Let the party begin right now!

He has made everything beautiful in its time. Also He has put eternity in their hearts, except that no one can find out the work that God does from beginning to end.

ECCLESIASTES 3:11 NKJV

Those who trust in the Lord are like Mount Zion, which cannot be moved but stands forever.

PSALM 125:1 NLV

Christ is the One Who gave us this New Way of Worship. All those who have been called by God may receive life that lasts forever just as He promised them. Christ bought us with His blood when He died for us. This made us free from our sins which we did under the Old Way of Worship.

HEBREWS 9:15 NLV

GOD IS MERCIFUL

*Whoever conceals their sins does not
prosper, but the one who confesses
and renounces them finds mercy.*

PROVERBS 28:13 NIV

If you've ever dieted, you know what it's like: You guard what you eat when you're with others—folks who know you're dieting. But sometimes, in the wee hours of the night, you sneak into the kitchen and grab a candy bar or a cookie. No one is watching, right?

We face that same temptation with sin. Sometimes we "sneak" a sinful action into our routine when we think it's safe. When no one's looking. But God is always looking, and our transgressions break His heart. Confessing our sin isn't easy, is it? Still, it's the only way to live in complete freedom. Hiding our transgressions is quite a temptation, but it's one we should avoid.

You've probably heard the expression all of your life: confession is good for the soul. Maybe it made no sense. To you, "confessing" meant getting in trouble. Aren't you glad you can safely confess your sins to God and receive grace and mercy in exchange? Now, that's a lovely trade-off!

And the LORD said, "I will cause all my goodness to pass in front of you, and I will proclaim my name, the LORD, in your presence. I will have mercy on whom I will have mercy, and I will have compassion on whom I will have compassion."

EXODUS 33:19 NIV

"For if you return to the LORD, your brethren and your children will be treated with compassion by those who lead them captive, so that they may come back to this land; for the LORD your God is gracious and merciful, and will not turn His face from you if you return to Him."

2 CHRONICLES 30:9 NKJV

For His merciful kindness is great toward us, and the truth of the LORD endures forever. Praise the LORD!

PSALM 117:2 NKJV

OUR SINS ARE WASHED AWAY

He has not punished us enough for all our sins.
He has not paid us back for all our wrong-doings.
PSALM 103:10 NLV

Have you ever been to Niagara Falls? Ever heard the roar of water as it rushes over the rocks, plummeting to the depths below? If so, then you have some inkling of what it's like to experience the "washing away" of sins. When we come to God with repentant hearts, He takes those things that have separated us from Him (sins, flaws, mess-ups) and rolls them over His version of Niagara Falls, never to be seen again.

If you're struggling to believe you've been forgiven, picture those sins plummeting into the rushing waters, gasping for air, and then finally disappearing downstream. They have no hold over you. They're gone forever. What joy, to know that God has washed us clean. We rise up out of the waters as new creations in Him. Praise the Lord! That's the best promise of all!

Peter replied, "Repent and be baptized, every one of you, in the name of Jesus Christ for the forgiveness of your sins. And you will receive the gift of the Holy Spirit."

ACTS 2:38 NIV

This is my blood of the covenant, which is poured out for many for the forgiveness of sins.

MATTHEW 26:28 NIV

"Therefore, my friends, I want you to know that through Jesus the forgiveness of sins is proclaimed to you."

ACTS 13:38 NIV

WHEN WE SERVE, WE PROSPER

*If they obey and serve him, they will
spend the rest of their days in prosperity
and their years in contentment.*

JOB 36:11 NIV

Most of us love to be served, though we probably wouldn't phrase it that way. And who would blame us? After all, we work really hard. It's nice to go out to a place where someone else prepares and delivers our food then cleans up our mess after the fact. It's great to stay in a hotel with maid service, a place where someone else makes the bed and washes the towels. We enjoy the little luxuries. Anyone would, right?

There's nothing wrong with being served, but the Bible makes it clear that listening to God's voice and then serving Him—with our worship, our kindness toward others, and so on—isn't just a good idea, it's a great idea!

Here's God's promise: when we serve, we will end our days in prosperity and pleasure. What a terrific way to wrap up your life, in such a joyous state.

Lead me, LORD, in your righteousness
because of my enemies—make
your way straight before me.

PSALM 5:8 NIV

Blessed are those who hunger
and thirst for righteousness,
for they will be filled.

MATTHEW 5:6 NIV

But seek first his kingdom and
his righteousness, and all these things
will be given to you as well.

MATTHEW 6:33 NIV

WE CAN MAKE HIS DEEDS KNOWN

*Give praise to the L*ORD*, proclaim his name;*
make known among the nations what he has done.
Sing to him, sing praise to him; tell of all his wonderful
acts. Glory in his holy name; let the hearts
*of those who seek the L*ORD *rejoice.*

1 CHRONICLES 16:8–10 NIV

Not everyone is called into the ministry. In fact, many of us shiver in our boots when we think of "spreading the Gospel" to our friends, neighbors, and people around the globe. The very idea terrifies us.

Here's some good news for you today, straight from God's Word. When we live a praise-filled life, when we continually call on God's name, we can't help but let others know what He's doing in our lives. We don't have to worry about "how" we tell them. Our very lives, loaded with praise and thanksgiving, will offer the testimony they need.

A celebratory life is a fine example for those who are wandering in grief and loneliness. They want what we have. So, offer up praise to Him today and then watch as others take notice of your relationship with the King of kings.

*Then the disciples went out and preached everywhere,
and the Lord worked with them and confirmed his
word by the signs that accompanied it.*
MARK 16:20 NIV

*He called you to this through our gospel,
that you might share in the glory of
our Lord Jesus Christ.*
2 THESSALONIANS 2:14 NIV

*Until I come, devote yourself to
the public reading of Scripture,
to preaching and to teaching.*
1 TIMOTHY 4:13 NIV

SIN IS NOT OUR MASTER

For sin shall no longer be your
master, because you are not under
the law, but under grace.

ROMANS 6:14 NIV

Imagine a poor slave girl bowing to her master's wants and wishes. She takes his abuse because she has no other choice. That's how it is when we allow sin to be "master" over us. We feel trapped in a life that we don't want. We wish for better things—freedom, peace, tranquility— but they seem elusive at best.

There's good news from the Word of God! When we come to Christ, when we accept His gift of salvation, we are no longer in chains (or bondage) to sin. Those shackles are broken the moment we give our hearts to the Lord. The only "master" in our lives is the one we've submitted our hearts to—the King of kings and Lord of lords. His grace and mercy are a lovely substitute for the abuse of the past. What joy!

For by grace you have been
saved through faith, and that not
of yourselves; it is the gift of God,
not of works, lest anyone should boast.

EPHESIANS 2:8–9 NKJV

And of His fullness we have all
received, and grace for grace.

JOHN 1:16 NKJV

And the Word became flesh and
dwelt among us, and we beheld His
glory, the glory as of the only begotten
of the Father, full of grace and truth.

JOHN 1:14 NKJV

NO MORE THAN WE CAN BEAR

No temptation has overtaken you except such as is common to man; but God is faithful, who will not allow you to be tempted beyond what you are able, but with the temptation will also make the way of escape, that you may be able to bear it.

1 CORINTHIANS 10:13 NKJV

Have you ever felt like the things you were facing were too much to bear? Like you wouldn't make it through? If so, today's scriptural promise should bring great comfort. God won't allow us to be tempted beyond what we can bear. Instead, He always provides a way of escape. He longs to see you walk in total freedom, above the temptations of this life.

So, look for His escape route today. Search it out. God will slip you through the secret passageway to freedom, peace, and joy, but you have to be on the lookout. Don't allow depression and anxiety to lock your knees. Stay flexible, and be willing to run toward the light when the moment comes.

Freedom is yours, but you must take action, trust in God's faithfulness and be prepared to make your escape!

"Forgive us our sins, for we also forgive everyone who sins against us. And lead us not into temptation."

LUKE 11:4 NIV

And don't let us yield to temptation, but rescue us from the evil one.

MATTHEW 6:13 NLT

"Why are you sleeping?" he asked them. "Get up and pray so that you will not fall into temptation."

LUKE 22:46 NIV

HE HEARS US

*This is the confidence we have in approaching God:
that if we ask anything according to his will, he hears
us. And if we know that he hears us—whatever we ask
—we know that we have what we asked of him.*

1 JOHN 5:14-15 NIV

If you've struggled with a hearing loss, you know how frustrating it can be. You have to ask people to repeat things often. Going to the movies is tough because you only catch about half the dialogue. People don't like to watch TV with you because you have to turn up the volume or use closed-captioning. Still, hearing is important!

Isn't it wonderful to know that God's hearing is impeccable? Not only does He hear your cries, He tunes in to your whispers. He even hears the silent cries of the heart—the ones you don't vocalize. His ear is ever-inclined toward you, waiting for your next breath, your next word.

Wow. Think about that. He's got billions of other

people to listen to, but still has time for your thoughts, your ideas, and your concerns. He hears you and He cares. What an amazing promise!

Evening, morning and noon I cry out
in distress, and he hears my voice.
PSALM 55:17 NIV

Then you will call my name.
You will come to me and pray to me,
and I will listen to you.
JEREMIAH 29:12 NCV

He fulfills the desires of those who fear
him; he hears their cry and saves them.
PSALM 145:19 NIV

PARDONED. . .AND HEALED

He forgives all my sins.
He heals all my sicknesses.
PSALM 103:3 NIRV

God longs to bless us. He's not content with just forgiving our sins so that we can (one day) have a great life in heaven. His goal is for us to live at peace right now, in this life. Many times we're bound up with internal and external pains and sicknesses. We feel like the struggles will never end.

Today's scriptural promise addresses that. He came to forgive (to pardon) and to heal. Sometimes we forget that we can ask God to heal our bodies, our minds, and our hearts. But He's still in the healing business. He longs to see us walk in wholeness.

We don't always understand how God's healing works, why some receive remarkable healings and others aren't healed until they get to heaven. But we are told to ask. So, perhaps today is your day. Are you sick? Hurting? Ask the Lord to heal then trust Him with the timing.

He sent out his word and healed them;
he rescued them from the grave.

Psalm 107:20 NIV

Let the wicked forsake their ways and the unrighteous
their thoughts. Let them turn to the Lord, and he will have
mercy on them, and to our God, for he will freely pardon.

Isaiah 55:7 NIV

Then Jesus said to him, "Get up
and go. Your faith has healed you."

Luke 17:19 NIRV

WE CAN BE REBORN

Jesus replied, "Very truly I tell you, no one can
see the kingdom of God unless they are born again."

JOHN 3:3 NIV

You must be born again. What do you think of when you read those words? Maybe you're like Nicodemus, a man in the Bible, who questioned Jesus when He said this. "Born again? What? I have to go back into my mother's womb and start over?"

Being born again isn't as complicated as all that. In fact, it's probably one of the simplest—but most profound—moves we can make. When we acknowledge our need for Christ, when we humble ourselves and cry out for forgiveness for the sins of the past, He grants not only mercy and grace, but a whole new life. Brand new. Old things passed away. A complete and total fresh start.

Born again. Our spirits are awakened from slumber, stepping into a brand-new existence, one that will last from now until eternity.

"You should not be surprised at my saying, 'You must be born again.' "

JOHN 3:7 NIV

For you have been born again, not of perishable seed, but of imperishable, through the living and enduring word of God.

1 PETER 1:23 NIV

They are reborn—not with a physical birth resulting from human passion or plan, but a birth that comes from God.

JOHN 1:13 NLT

HE WON'T FAIL US

*"Be strong and courageous. Do not be afraid
or terrified because of them, for the LORD your God goes
with you; he will never leave you nor forsake you."*

DEUTERONOMY 31:6 NIV

Have you ever failed a test in school? It's bound to happen, sooner or later, whether we're talking about school tests or life tests. They're hard, after all. And we're not expected to sail through every one. That's why they're called *tests*!

There is only One who has never failed a test, and He's proven Himself faithful in every area. Jesus won't fail you. In fact, He can't fail.

Ponder that for a moment. "God won't fail me." Repeat those words several times in a row. They're true, you know. This scriptural promise brings such comfort, especially when we're facing a trial. You might not pass this test, but Christ will. It's impossible for Him to get a failing grade, no matter how much you've messed up. So, count on Him to make things right. He will. Just trust Him.

Well then, has God failed to fulfill his promise
to Israel? No, for not all who are born into the
nation of Israel are truly members of God's people!

ROMANS 9:6 NLT

Don't love money; be satisfied with what
you have. For God has said, "I will never
fail you. I will never abandon you."

HEBREWS 13:5 NLT

"Blessed be the LORD, who has given rest
to His people Israel, according to all that
He promised. There has not failed one word of
all His good promise, which He promised
through His servant Moses."

1 KINGS 8:56 NKJV

GOD FREELY BESTOWS HIS GRACE

To the praise of his glorious grace,
which he has freely given us in the One he loves.

EPHESIANS 1:6 NIV

When you love someone, you want to bless them. Take your children or grandchildren, for instance. Love compels you to "do" for them, even when it's a sacrifice. Even when they've misbehaved.

The same is true with God. He loves us so much that He wants to freely bestow His love, His grace, and His mercy on us, even when we don't deserve it. That's why it's called "grace," after all—it's God's unmerited favor.

Here's the best news of all: the Lord freely gives. That means He's not standing with hand outstretched, waiting for us to somehow pay Him back. His grace is a free gift, though it cost His Son dearly. So, we can't take advantage of this amazing grace. We must treasure it as the gift it is.

For the law was given through Moses;
grace and truth came through Jesus Christ.
JOHN 1:17 NIV

"Now I commit you to God and to the
word of his grace, which can build you up
and give you an inheritance among all
those who are sanctified."
ACTS 20:32 NIV

However, I consider my life worth
nothing to me; my only aim is to finish the
race and complete the task the Lord Jesus
has given me—the task of testifying to the
good news of God's grace.
ACTS 20:24 NIV

WE CAN BELIEVE WHEN WE PRAY

*"Have faith in God," Jesus answered. "Truly I tell you,
if anyone says to this mountain, 'Go, throw yourself
into the sea,' and does not doubt in their heart but
believes that what they say will happen, it will be
done for them. Therefore I tell you, whatever you
ask for in prayer, believe that you have
received it, and it will be yours."*

MARK 11:22–24 NIV

Imagine you were a small child at your mama's knee.
You repeatedly asked for something—say, a special
treat—only to be told, "No!" every single time. How
depressing, to always receive a negative response. After a
while you would stop asking, wouldn't you?

Here's the good news about your heavenly Father.
He enjoys pouring out blessing upon blessing. Today's
verse advises us to believe when we ask. Of course, we
have to ask Him for sensible things, but He enjoys the
smile on our face when He says "Yes" to our requests.
So, don't be afraid to make your requests known. And

while you're at it, why not stretch your faith and ask Him for something that seems bigger than usual. You might be surprised if He comes through for you, but He won't be.

Believe. Such a small word, but such a big action.

I would have lost heart, unless I had believed that I would
see the goodness of the LORD in the land of the living.

PSALM 27:13 NKJV

Then Jesus declared, "I am the bread of life.
Whoever comes to me will never go hungry,
and whoever believes in me will never be thirsty."

JOHN 6:35 NIV

The Lord's hand was with them, and a great number of
people believed and turned to the Lord.

ACTS 11:21 NIV

THIRSTY NO MORE!

For he satisfies the thirsty and
fills the hungry with good things.

PSALM 107:9 NIV

Have you ever pictured yourself going without food or water for an extended period of time? Maybe trekking across the desert without adequate provisions? Thirst is a powerful force, and so is hunger. Both of them can drive you to your knees, and/or drive you to do out-of-the-norm things.

It's such a blessing to realize that God won't leave us hungry and thirsty. When we come to Him—our spiritual bellies empty—He fills us. How? With His love, His peace, His joy, His provision. We don't walk away from our God-encounters saying things like, "Man, I wish He cared about me," or, "I wish God understood all the things I need/want." He gets it, and He cares.

Maybe you're feeling empty today. Run to Him. Lay it out there. Tell Him about the aches, the loneliness, and the pain. He will sweep in and fill you like you've never been filled before. You won't leave empty, that's for sure!

I spread out my hands to you;
I thirst for you like a parched land.

PSALM 143:6 NIV

As the deer pants for the water brooks,
so my soul pants for You, O God.

PSALM 42:1 NASB

For He has satisfied the thirsty soul,
and the hungry soul He has
filled with what is good.

PSALM 107:9 NASB

EAGLE-LIKE CHANGES

Who satisfies your years with good things,
so that your youth is renewed like the eagle.

PSALM 103:5 NASB

Eagles go through a wide variety of changes—or trans-formations—in their lives. First their white down changes to gray. Then darker-colored feathers begin to grow. The beautiful bird doesn't reach its full plumage until it's five years old. Every step of the way, God gives the eagle what he needs.

The same is true with us, God's children. As we grow and develop in our faith, we go through a variety of necessary changes. Some (similar to shedding down and growing feathers) might seem difficult, but God knows what we need when we need it.

Yes, we will go through odd seasons where we have to trust Him more than usual. This is inevitable as we grow and develop. But God is faithful and will satisfy us with good things along the way. We can trust Him, just as that beautiful eagle trusts that he will one day take flight.

Anyone who gives a lot will succeed.
Anyone who renews others will be renewed.
PROVERBS 11:25 NIRV

We don't give up. Our bodies are becoming
weaker and weaker. But our spirits
are being renewed day by day.
2 CORINTHIANS 4:16 NIRV

My brother, we both belong to the Lord. So I wish
I could receive some benefit from you. Renew my heart.
We know that Christ is the one who really renews it.
PHILEMON 1:20 NIRV

GOD'S COVENANT

"For the LORD your God is a compassionate God;
He will not fail you nor destroy you nor forget the
covenant with your fathers which He swore to them."

DEUTERONOMY 4:31 NASB

Perhaps you read today's verse and scratch your head, confused. The word "covenant" makes no sense to you. What is a covenant anyway?

If you've ever entered into an agreement with someone, (say, you purchased a home from a lender) you've entered into "covenant" with them. This means you are bound together by your agreement. You've taken a pledge to pay the money back. Maybe you've even put down earnest money as a guarantee.

God has entered into a covenant with us. He has agreed to stick with us, no matter what. What do we agree to? To walk in relationship with His Son, Jesus, all the days of our life. This agreement is an "understanding" between our Creator and us: we're linked. Bonded. Held together—and all through the work of Jesus on the cross.

I will establish my covenant as an everlasting covenant
between me and you and your descendants after you for
the generations to come, to be your God and
the God of your descendants after you.

GENESIS 17:7 NIV

He provides food for those who fear him;
he remembers his covenant forever.

PSALM 111:5 NIV

He remembers His covenant forever,
the word which He commanded,
for a thousand generations.

PSALM 105:8 NKJV

I CAN SLEEP IN PEACE

In peace I will lie down and sleep,
for you alone, LORD, make me dwell in safety.

PSALM 4:8 NIV

Remember that wonderful Christmas song "Silent Night"? The gentle lullaby has survived for hundreds of years, in part because of its lovely melody, and in part because of the simplicity of the lyrics.

The "sleep in heavenly peace" part resonates with many of us because we wish we had that option. We're so busy juggling job, family, meals, dishes, laundry, and so forth, that we're wound up like a clock by the time we finally tumble into bed. Many of us stay awake, troubled by financial issues, relational problems, and a thousand other things. We just can't seem to rest our minds, no matter how exhausted our bodies!

Here's a wonderful scriptural promise: When we "dwell" in God's safety (resting in the security that He's got things handled) we can lie down and sleep in peace. No troubling thoughts. No tossing and turning. Just sweet, joyous sleep!

When you lie down, you will not be afraid;
when you lie down, your sleep will be sweet.
PROVERBS 3:24 NIV

Yes, I must find my rest in God.
He is the God who gives me hope.
PSALM 62:5 NIRV

"Come to me, all you who are tired and
are carrying heavy loads. I will give you rest."
MATTHEW 11:28 NIRV

GOD WILL VINDICATE

*When I awake, I will be satisfied
with seeing your likeness.*

PSALM 17:15 NIV

Picture a boxer in the ring. He's been knocked down, maybe even knocked out. Everything is a fuzzy mess. He can't distinguish one thing from another. In the back of his mind he knows that his opponent must have hit him pretty hard or he wouldn't be lying on the floor.

Then, breaking through the fog and haze, he clamps eyes on the Lord. Not his opponent. Not the crowd, but Jesus. Wow.

That's kind of like what we go through when we've been badly hurt. Nothing makes sense in the moment, but when we "come to" (see things more clearly after-the-fact) one Person is in our line of sight: Jesus. When we focus on Him, when we remember that He is the One who will vindicate, we don't have to be afraid. We also don't have to come up with a strategy for taking out our opponent. All we have to do is look into Jesus' eyes and trust that He's got this.

Let the LORD judge the peoples. Vindicate
me, LORD, according to my righteousness,
according to my integrity, O Most High.
PSALM 7:8 NIV

I cry out to God Most High,
to God, who vindicates me.
PSALM 57:2 NIV

The LORD has vindicated us. Come,
let us announce in Jerusalem everything
the LORD our God has done.
JEREMIAH 51:10 NLT

ASK, SEEK, KNOCK

"Ask, and it will be given to you; seek, and you will find;
knock, and it will be opened to you. For everyone
who asks receives, and he who seeks finds,
and to him who knocks it will be opened."

MATTHEW 7:7–8 NKJV

Remember what you were like as a kid? Most children are loaded with questions: "When are we going to get there?" "Will you buy me that toy?" "What am I getting for Christmas?" "Can I stay up late tonight?" "Can I have some candy?"

We weren't afraid to ask. . .anything!

God wants us to approach Him with that same type of boldness. We're to come to His throne room with a childlike sense of expectation. That's why He tells us to ask. To seek. To knock. Instead of timidly approaching our heavenly Father, we need to come skipping like a little child into His presence with anticipation bubbling up inside of us.

Knock on the door, child of God! Your Father is standing on the other side, ready to bless you!

"You can pray for anything, and if you have faith, you will receive it."

MATTHEW 21:22 NLT

Therefore I tell you, whatever you ask for in prayer, believe that you have received it, and it will be yours.

MARK 11:24 NIV

The poor will see and be glad—you who seek God, may your hearts live!

PSALM 69:32 NIV

SAFETY IS MINE

The name of the LORD is a strong fortress;
the godly run to him and are safe.
PROVERBS 18:10 NLT

Remember the games you used to play as a kid? Most of them involved a "base" (a safe place) where you would run. You would move as fast as possible to get there.

There's still a "base" that you can run to, one where you're completely and totally safe—from harm, from pain, from distress. That base is the Lord Jesus. His name (ah, that name—Jesus!) is a strong tower. If you think of it in fairy-tale terms, it's that high place where you look out over the kingdom, free from worries. God bids us to run into that place so that we can experience complete safety and provision.

You are a daughter of the King! So, run into the safety of His arms today. Don't wait. He's longing to prove that you can be truly safe in Him.

The LORD rescues the godly;
he is their fortress in times of trouble.

PSALM 37:39 NLT

The LORD is my light and my salvation—
so why should I be afraid? The LORD is
my fortress, protecting me from danger,
so why should I tremble?

PSALM 27:1 NLT

The LORD Almighty is with us;
the God of Jacob is our fortress.

PSALM 46:7 NIV

RIGHTEOUSNESS IS REWARDED

"Surely there is a reward for the righteous;
surely He is God who judges in the earth."

PSALM 58:11 NKJV

The Bible is clear that we don't earn our salvation by doing good works. By the same token, we are saved to do good works. When it comes right down to it, our "acts of righteousness" (godly living) should come as naturally to us as breathing. If our hearts are linked to Christ, we should long to please Him in all we do, the big and small things of life.

There is a reward for righteous living: a sense of satisfaction. When we're pleasing our heavenly Father with our actions, we're satisfied from the inside out. We're content in the fact that we're putting a smile on His face and bringing Him pleasure. Every little child wants to make his or her Daddy happy after all.

We're not always "righteous" of course. Still, when we do make good choices, the world is watching, and God is smiling down on us. What a joyous way to live.

*The L*ORD *has rewarded me according*
to my righteousness, according to
my cleanness in his sight.

2 SAMUEL 22:25 NIV

*The L*ORD *loves righteousness and justice;*
the earth is full of his unfailing love.

PSALM 33:5 NIV

He will bring forth your righteousness as the
light and your judgment as the noonday.

PSALM 37:6 NASB

GOD CAN TEACH ME TO BE MERCIFUL

Therefore be merciful,
just as your Father also is merciful.
LUKE 6:36 NKJV

Oh, how we long to be merciful as God is merciful. And we do our best. . .on most days. Then, along comes a day when someone—or something—hits us the wrong way. We're frustrated. Angry. And so, we snap. We don't mean to, but our desire to show mercy evaporates in an instant. Sure, we still hope and pray others will show us mercy, but reciprocating seems elusive at best.

How does God teach us to be merciful? By example! He picks us up and dusts us off after every tumble. No pointing fingers. No "Why didn't you do better?" No "Next time I'm gonna give you a spanking!" Nope. He simply brushes us off, gives us a holy hug, and leaves us feeling convinced that we are still loved, no matter how messy our flaws.

When we've received this kind of mercy time and again, it gets easier to extend it to others. Sure, we're on a learning curve, but sooner or later mercy will be a part of our makeup, something that comes as naturally as breathing.

His miracles are unforgettable.
The LORD is kind and merciful.

PSALM 111:4 NCV

"For I will be merciful to their iniquities,
and I will remember their sins no more."

HEBREWS 8:12 NASB

"Blessed are the merciful,
for they shall receive mercy."

MATTHEW 5:7 NASB

WISDOM MAKES US STRONG

A wise man is strong, yes,
a man of knowledge increases strength.

PROVERBS 24:5 NKJV

Do you remember watching Popeye the Sailor Man? One can of spinach, and. . .bam! His muscles plumped up, his strength increased, and he garnered the courage to face whatever enemy happened to be standing in his path.

There's no magic can of spinach for us to swallow, but today's scripture offers another suggestion: wisdom. If we spend our days growing in godly wisdom, we increase in strength. Like Popeye, we garner strength to whip our enemies, though not necessarily physical ones. Strong in spirit, we can defeat the enemy of our soul when he tries to attack.

So, what are you waiting for? Grab a can of wisdom—aka, the Bible—and eat up! Before long you'll be stronger than ever.

He gives strength to the weary, and to
him who lacks might He increases power.

ISAIAH 40:29 NASB

The angel answered and said to her,
"The Holy Spirit will come upon you, and the
power of the Most High will overshadow
you; and for that reason the holy Child
shall be called the Son of God."

LUKE 1:35 NASB

But if any of you needs wisdom, you should
ask God for it. He is generous to everyone and
will give you wisdom without criticizing you.

JAMES 1:5 NCV

WE CAN PROSPER

*Beloved, I pray that you may prosper in all things
and be in health, just as your soul prospers.*

3 JOHN 1:2 NKJV

What does it mean to prosper? To some, it might mean acquiring lots of money. To others, "prospering" simply means having their needs met. If you look up the word *prosper* you will see that the definition includes the word *success*. When you're successful, you're making progress, moving from Point A to Point B, and so on. This puts a whole new spin on the word *prosper,* doesn't it?

If you are in a prosperous season, likely it has more to do with your spiritual condition than anything you could acquire with money. And when your soul (heart, mind, emotions) is prospering, you can count on the fact that your health will follow. So, if you want to be in great health, make sure your soul is successful. There's really only one way to accomplish this—stick close to God. Read His Word. Live by His precepts. Then watch as "success" follows.

The lions may grow weak and hungry,
*but those who seek the L*ORD *lack no good thing.*

PSALM 34:10 NIV

If they obey and serve Him, they shall spend their
days in prosperity, and their years in pleasures.

JOB 36:11 NKJV

He shall be like a tree planted by the rivers of water,
that brings forth its fruit in its season, whose leaf also shall
not wither; and whatever he does shall prosper.

PSALM 1:3 NKJV

WE WON'T DROWN

But now the Lord Who made you, O Jacob, and He Who made you, O Israel, says, "Do not be afraid. For I have bought you and made you free. I have called you by name. You are Mine! When you pass through the waters, I will be with you. When you pass through the rivers, they will not flow over you. When you walk through the fire, you will not be burned. The fire will not destroy you."

ISAIAH 43:1–2 NLV

If you've ever been trapped in deep water, you know the panic of trying to hold your head up. One wrong move and you could go under for good. Now picture yourself wearing a life vest, one that keeps you afloat no matter how much you panic. That's what it's like with God—He's the best life vest ever!

Today's scriptural promise is a doozy! We can go through high waters and not drown. Amazing. We can go through the fire and come out without the smell of smoke in our hair. What does this mean? We face very difficult seasons. We're afraid they will take us down, that we'll never recover. But when we belong to God, we're never adrift without provision. His "life jacket" is always there, holding us up.

Yes, we go through rough seasons, but we will not drown, even when the waters rage around us. Praise God!

The LORD is my rock and my fortress and my deliverer; my God, my strength, in whom I will trust; my shield and the horn of my salvation, my stronghold.

PSALM 18:2 NKJV

I will say to the Lord, "You are my safe and strong place, my God, in Whom I trust."

PSALM 91:2 NLV

For You have been a safe place for me, a tower of strength where I am safe from those who fight against me.

PSALM 61:3 NLV

GREATER WORKS

"Most assuredly, I say to you, he who believes in Me, the works that I do he will do also; and greater works than these he will do, because I go to My Father."

John 14:12 NKJV

Today's verse is a tough one for many believers. Many of us read those words and say, "What? I'm going to do greater works than Jesus?" Seems almost blasphemous, doesn't it? After all, Jesus raised the dead, healed the sick, breathed life into situations, but He was—and is—the Son of God!

What if you had the faith to believe that nothing was impossible? Would it change anything? Would you approach the situations around you differently? Why not take a day or two and ask God for the "extreme" faith required to believe today's promise. Ask Him to fill you with such great "belief in the impossible" that everything you encounter seems possible. Doable.

The Lord might just use you to affect your world in a major way. It could happen. Brace yourself, because this is one promise that will leave you completely, radically changed.

For we are His workmanship, created in Christ Jesus for good works, which God prepared beforehand so that we would walk in them.

EPHESIANS 2:10 NASB

For the Father loves the Son and shows him all he does. Yes, and he will show him even greater works than these, so that you will be amazed.

JOHN 5:20 NIV

The people were amazed and said to each other, "What does this mean? With authority and power he commands evil spirits, and they come out."

LUKE 4:36 NCV

WE HAVE AN INHERITANCE

In Him also we have obtained an inheritance,
being predestined according to the purpose of Him
who works all things according to the counsel of His will.

EPHESIANS 1:11 NKJV

Have you ever inherited something special from a relative? Maybe you've got Aunt Mary's journal or your mom's favorite brooch. Maybe you were blessed to receive your grandfather's Bible or your dad's class ring. Such gifts can truly be treasures.

As wonderful as those items might be, we have an inheritance that is far greater. God has gifted us with eternal life. He "chose" us, even before the foundation of the world. Wow!

This "inheritance" was the gift that His Son, Jesus, left us when He died on the cross for our sins. We can take hold of this treasure right now—today—and it will change our very lives, not just now, but for all eternity. Eternal life. And we've been chosen to have it. Talk about a gift passed down from one generation to another!

*Whatever you do, work heartily, as for the Lord and
not for men, knowing that from the Lord you will
receive the inheritance as your reward.
You are serving the Lord Christ.*
COLOSSIANS 3:23–24 ESV

*So that being justified by his grace we might become
heirs according to the hope of eternal life.*
TITUS 3:7 ESV

*Blessed is the nation whose God
is the LORD, the people whom He has
chosen for His own inheritance.*
PSALM 33:12 NASB

GOD'S SON CHANGED EVERYTHING

For to us a child is born, to us a son is given, and the government will be on his shoulders. And he will be called Wonderful Counselor, Mighty God, Everlasting Father, Prince of Peace. Of the greatness of his government and peace there will be no end. He will reign on David's throne and over his kingdom, establishing and upholding it with justice and righteousness from that time on and forever.

ISAIAH 9:6–7 NIV

God's Son—Jesus—changed everything. Think about that for a moment. The little baby in the manger changed history, changed the course of the church, and has changed your very life. Your family will never be the same. The world will never be the same. God's people will never be the same. . .and all because of Jesus.

Maybe you've struggled to understand the relevance of Jesus Christ in today's world. Maybe you look around at the troubles in your country, your home, your personal life, and wonder, "Is He still changing things today?"

The answer is a resounding "Yes!" Invite Him to be the very center of the "thing" (relationship, problem, issue) you're facing. From that pivotal spot, Jesus is free to blow the winds in a completely different direction. Keep Him in His rightful place, then watch change come.

He will be great and will be called the Son of the Most High; and the Lord God will give Him the throne of His father David.

LUKE 1:32 NASB

The angel answered and said to her, "The Holy Spirit will come upon you, and the power of the Most High will overshadow you; and for that reason the holy Child shall be called the Son of God."

LUKE 1:35 NASB

And they all said, "Are You the Son of God, then?" And He said to them, "Yes, I am."

LUKE 22:70 NASB

SEEK HIM, FIND HIM

I love those who love me,
and those who seek me find me.
PROVERBS 8:17 NCV

Remember scavenger hunts? You went door to door, asking for items on a list. You searched and searched, from home to home, until you found everything you needed. Then you took your items back to your house, hopefully arriving before the others, so that you could win the game.

Sometimes searching for God is a bit like going on a scavenger hunt. When you're going through a tough time, you cry out to Him, but He doesn't always answer right away or in the way you'd hoped.

It's not that the Lord is hiding from you. He's right there, as always. Sometimes it's just a season. He holds back, waiting for a change in your heart. Or He speaks in a still, small voice, one that requires you to be very quiet in order to hear Him. Keep seeking. Don't give up, no matter how quiet the season. He's right there, waiting to guide you onward.

Be glad that you are his; let those
*who seek the L*ord *be happy.*

Psalm 105:3 NCV

My heart says of you, "Seek his face!"
*Your face, L*ord*, I will seek.*

Psalm 27:8 NIV

But may all who seek you rejoice and
be glad in you; may those who long for your
*saving help always say, "The L*ord *is great!"*

Psalm 40:16 NIV

GOD IS BIGGER

"I have told you these things, so that in me you may have peace. In this world you will have trouble. But take heart! I have overcome the world."

JOHN 16:33 NIV

Remember when you were a kid, how someone's size could intimidate you? A bully seemed meaner because he was bigger than the other guys. And if he had an older, bigger brother, look out! You really had something to worry about!

Here's good news: God is the biggest of the big. No one can outsize Him. He's bigger than the biggest big brother. Because He's bigger than any foe you could possibly face, you have nothing to fear. He wants to replace your anxieties with His peace—the kind of peace that says, "Hey, calm down! I've got this. Let me handle it for you."

Sure, you'll still have troubles. Bullies will raise their ugly fists. But if you will step aside and let God handle them all, those troubles will resolve themselves in a hurry.

*"They will fight against you but will
not overcome you, for I am with you and
will rescue you," declares the L*ORD*.*

J*EREMIAH* 1:19 NIV

*Such people will not be overcome
by evil. Those who are righteous
will be long remembered.*

P*SALM* 112:6 NLT

*For You have armed me with strength
for the battle; You have subdued under
me those who rose up against me.*

P*SALM* 18:39 NKJV

PARDONED BY GOD

Let the wicked forsake his way, and the unrighteous man
his thoughts; let him return to the LORD, and He will
have mercy on him; and to our God,
for He will abundantly pardon.

ISAIAH 55:7 NKJV

Imagine for a minute that you are in a courtroom, accused of a crime. It's a crime you're truly guilty of. After a moment's thought, the judge declares your innocence.

Really? Innocent? You know in your heart that you're not, but the man in the robe is ready to pardon you, no questions asked. You can go free. At first it seems surreal. Then, as your eyes adjust to the sunshine outside the courtroom, you realize just how blessed you are to be given a second chance.

When God sent His Son, Jesus, to the cross to die for your sins, He (symbolically) sat across the table from you and pardoned you from your sins. Suddenly the things you'd done wrong—the lies, the pain you'd caused others—were washed away. Not only that, your pardon included an all-expenses paid trip into eternity!

For He made Him who knew no sin to be sin for us,
that we might become the righteousness of God in Him.

2 Corinthians 5:21 NKJV

Your word I have hidden in my heart,
that I might not sin against You.

Psalm 119:11 NKJV

"Why do you not pardon my offenses and
forgive my sins? For I will soon lie down in the dust;
you will search for me, but I will be no more."

Job 7:21 NIV